Redefining Church Membership

From Myth to Ministry

JOHN S. POWERS

Leadership and Adult Publishing
LifeWay Church Resources
One LifeWay Plaza
Nashville, TN 37234-0175

ISBN 0-6330-1759-0

This book is a text for one Christian Growth Study Plan course:
LS-0017 Church Leadership

Dewey Decimal Classification: 254
Subject Heading: CHURCH MEMBERSHIP

Unless otherwise indicated, all Scripture quotations are from the
NEW AMERICAN STANDARD BIBLE (NASB)
© Copyright The Lockman Foundation, 1960, 1962, 1963, 1968, 1971, 1973,
1975, 1977, 1995. Used by permission.

To order additional copies of this resource: WRITE LifeWay Church Resources
Customer Service; One LifeWay Plaza; Nashville, TN 37234-0113;
FAX order to (615) 251-5933; PHONE (800) 458-2772;
E-MAIL to *customerservice@lifeway.com;* ORDER ONLINE at *www.lifeway.com;*
or VISIT the LifeWay Christian Store serving you.

Printed in the United States of America

LifeWay Church Resources, a division of
LifeWay Christian Resources
of the Southern Baptist Convention
One LifeWay Plaza
Nashville, TN 37234-0175

This book is dedicated to:

Connie Powers

*Each day of our twenty-seven years together
has deepened my passionate love for you.
I look forward to growing old together!*

Nathan Powers

*My precious son,
it is my prayer that you may reach
your generation for our Lord Jesus.
I am so proud of you!*

CONTENTS

Acknowledgments

Obviously, I am like a turtle sitting on top of a fence post. I did not get here alone. I had a lot of help from a cadre of caring mentors and co-laborers. I must express my deepest appreciation to them. When I am around these major-league athletes, I feel like a decent softball player who has bribed his way into the World Series. These people are Rolex watches. I am a Timex. The Lord continues to use each of them to touch my life and change me forever. The first is my father, Charles Powers. Thanks, Dad, for investing years of your life in me. Making my primary mentor proud remains a priority for me.

Thank you, Ansel Baker, my first pastoral mentor. You helped me see that ministry can be broad and effective. Sincere gratitude to you, my brother and dearest friend, Dr. Malcolm McDow. Our many conversations over the years have taught me how to think like a theologian. I hope that I do. Thank you, Glenn Sheppard; you continue to challenge me. Your passion for Jesus has impacted me beyond words. You introduced me to the power of intercession.

My limited vocabulary cannot express adequately how I feel about my father in the ministry, Dr. James T. Draper, Jr. Time after time you have chosen to overlook my childish behavior and loved me. Truly, iron is sharpening iron. To Dr. Jay Strack, my beloved friend and encourager, many times you have come alongside me with fresh winds of insight seasoned with humor. Our Lord used you to rescue me from drowning in some rough waters of ministry.

Several friends have been invaluable in completing this project. Ralph Burrage, through his wisdom and ministry savvy, has kept me sharp. Helen Spore's writing skills and keen eye have taken my thoughts and made them readable. My administrative assistant, Diane Styron, is one of the greatest blessings in my ministry. I would be remiss if I forgot to express my appreciation to Mark Marshall and Norma (J.J.) Goldman in the LifeWay Church Resources division of LifeWay Christian Resources. Without Mark's visionary assistance and J.J.'s strong editorial skills, this work might never have been completed.

Finally, thank you for reading this book. May the Lord richly bless your ministry with His burden to make a difference in this generation of lost souls. May you be found faithful as you finish the Great Commission task through the local church.

THE TIME HAS COME!

Everyone should be passionate about something. Three things that stimulate me beyond my limited vocabulary are my family, my hobby, and my vocation. This attempt at putting thoughts on a page is dedicated to my family. Connie, my faithful and dear wife of almost twenty-seven years, and Nathan, our teenage son, are the two most incredible people on the planet! Thinking of these two people is like adding sugar to my coffee. When I see them, reflect on them, or pray for them, a smile explodes from inside to the outside. Containing my personal passion for my wife and son is like standing in the ocean and trying to stop the waves.

Playing golf is my favorite hobby. Actually, calling golf my hobby is possibly the greatest understatement since God told Noah it was going to rain a little! It seems the only piece of equipment I have yet to purchase is one of those sweaters that says, "Will Golf for Food." Honestly, being on the PGA tour would fulfill a lifelong dream were it not for the fact that I stand too close to the ball . . . after I hit it! In my humble opinion, there is no such thing as a bad day on a golf course. There are good and better days, but no bad ones.

My life's work, my vocational burn, is within the local church. I love the Lord. I love His people and have given my entire life to fulfilling my call in ministry. Ever since I established a relationship with Jesus Christ at the tender age of sixteen, my journey of faith has centered in the local church and her work. Allow me to use two different kinds of imagery to describe my passionate feelings about the body of Christ as well as my role within her.

First, and for the most part, the local church reminds me of a critically ill patient with multiple health issues. I have a dear friend, John Nelson, who serves our community as a fireman and a paramedic. From time to time, I volunteer to join this ex-Marine for several hours of an evening shift. That means I go wherever he goes, including ambulance rides to various emergency rooms throughout Hampton Roads, Virginia. In the past few years, I have observed him as he handled many different kinds of medical treatments ranging from simple ankle injuries to major heart attacks.

One emergency call stands out in my mind. A middle-aged man was struggling with congestive heart failure. When John and I entered his home, we could not help but notice the yards of oxygen tubing stretched across the tile floor and dozens of medicine bottles lined up on the kitchen counter. That fellow had multiple medical problems and was minutes from death. After John stabilized the patient, he rushed him to a local hospital. At the emergency room, a young doctor who specialized in congestive heart problems treated this ailing man. The doctor and my friend, John, saved the man's life! Like the doctor, I view one of my roles within the local church more along the lines of a specialist rather than a generalist. The "church patient" has many needs and my passion is to focus upon a selected few of those needs. Many other people in the kingdom are equipped to handle other pressing needs of equal importance, but the passion of this soul-winner is to equip the saints to do the work of ministry.

A second image that conveys my heart for ministry is a telescope. For years I have enjoyed looking into the heavens to observe the movement of the planets. All my life, I have viewed astronomical features with the naked eye. This is doubly difficult because I am legally blind in one eye. In fact, my glasses are so thick that when I look at a map, I can see people waving! If the corrective lens of my glasses get any thicker, I will be able to see into next week! You can "see" the physical problem I have (pun intended).

In my opinion, the movie *The Christmas Story* is a classic. It tells the saga of Ralphie who wanted a BB gun so badly he could taste it. That's the way I felt about a telescope. For years, I investigated telescopes. I even considered joining an astronomy "star party" group. When my staff surprised me with a telescope for a Christmas gift, I could not wait for the sun to set. On that cold Christmas night, I set this scientific toy in the center of my deck and focused on the largest feature in the crisp, clear night sky — the moon. Like you, I have seen the moon. But have you really *seen* the moon? On that night, its craters seemed so close I felt I could reach out and touch them. Viewed through a telescope, lunar mountains stand out in sharp contrast to the smoother terrain of the moon. It was a Kodak moment!

Just as the lens of a telescope allows a well-trained scientist and a novice like me to view faraway objects clearly, the Lord continues His work of bringing my life into focus. His plan is sharpening my life into a lucid picture. My passion is encouraging believers to connect to the life of a local church. So I have decided to focus our mental telescopes on what it really means to bestow the title "member" upon a believer in your church or mine.

Effective ministry within the local church demands proper assimilation of people. For years, I have struggled with ideology that fosters a seemingly unbreakable cycle that promotes nominal behavior by church members. I have wrestled with an unmoving mind-set that has been formed in the concrete of tradition. I have been frustrated with mythological thinking of believers, including well-intended seminary professors, pastors, staff members, deacons, and everyday members. My own presuppositions about church membership have sickened me at times.

By nature I am an upbeat, positive individual with a "can-do" spirit. I don't understand people who feel it is their calling to habitually criticize without providing solutions to problems. It is my opinion that the typical church member is mishandled. As a result of our mishandling, many believers are forfeited and forgotten. Too many people become casualties of ministry. And it's out of this burden that I attempt to provide solutions with practical steps to overcoming this growing crisis. The results of local churches seem to bear out the fact that, generally, what we are doing is not working. Allow me to probe the patient for a moment.

- Are our churches developing fully devoted followers of Jesus or members who are casual and comfortable in their faith?
- Is there a system that expects members to participate in the life of a local church, or does the system encourage them to freelance and remain unaccountable?
- Can the body of Christ make the needed impact in the face of unprecedented ministry opportunity with the level of loyalty we see in the typical church member?

The more I have learned, the less I truly know. I have many questions and am now ready to begin the search for answers. Why? I am reminded of an old Chinese proverb that defines insanity as "doing the same things we've always done and expecting different results."

The purpose of this book is to find answers that will truly bring about change. I realize that being transparent comes at great expense, but the time has come to do so. Sometimes I can't decide whether I am a dreamer or a world-class fool. One thing is true. The time has come to lay some issues on the table that will evoke a change in the way we view church membership.

Our goal is to produce fruitful believers with biblical behavior. First, I want to identify the problem by examining philosophical mountains built by mythological thinking. Then we will investigate different myths that emanate from the mindset of typical believers. The final chapter discusses how pastors and church leaders can develop an action plan to address and change from this mythological thinking to a biblical view of the New Testament church.

CHAPTER 1

Give Me This Mountain!

*U*ltimately, whether or not a church demonstrates the care and love of Christ boils down to its vision and structure. Know what you believe God wants you to do, develop the organizational framework so it can happen, and some amazing things will result. That's how the business community operates. If they can do it, why aren't we? We have God, and they have the dollar; surely God is a more durable and compelling motivation than the dollar! [1]

Caleb is one of the great Bible characters. Like a stone skipping across tranquil water, his story glides over the pages of history. His life impacted a nation that needed strong leadership. Let's dig into some scenes of his life for a few moments to gain insights from this man of God.

Caleb was eighty-five years old when he stepped out of the ranks to claim an inheritance the Lord had promised him forty-five years earlier. At Kadesh-barnea the Israelites stood on the very border of God's promise. But like every generation, numbered in the ranks that day were unbelievers who hindered the progress of God's people at every turn. You may remember that Caleb was one of twelve who had been commissioned to take a six-week inspection tour of the Promised Land and report back their findings. On that fateful day two reports were given. When the dust cleared from the first church business meeting, a majority saw giants and said, "We can't." But then came the minority report from Joshua and Caleb. They admitted the existence of obstacles. They saw the walled cities and measured the strong men who stood upon them. Alan Redpath notes,

> They had seen all that the majority had seen, with this difference: the majority measured the giants against their own strength; Caleb and Joshua measured the giants against God. The majority trembled; the two triumphed. The majority had great giants but a little God. Caleb had a great God and little giants.[2]

With a voice of faith Caleb attempted to sway public opinion by proclaiming to the people of Israel, "Guys, we can eat their lunch!" But the fourteenth chapter of Numbers records a decision that would haunt these Israelites for the next forty years. Their lack of faith came at a great price, for the Lord refused to give this generation the Promised Land — that is, except for Joshua and Caleb, about whom the Lord testified,

> *But My servant Caleb, because he has had a different spirit and has followed Me fully, I will bring into the land which he entered, and his descendants shall take possession of it* (Numbers 14:24).

Forty-five years later, Caleb, who believed the promises of God are not empty theory but a precious reality, stood before Joshua to lay claim to his land saying, "Give me this mountain" (Joshua 14:12). This rugged terrain is called Hebron and is the same site where Abraham had pitched his tent. It was at Hebron that God and Abraham met face to face. Hebron was the place where God gave the Promised Land to Abraham. Now the title deed belonged to Caleb! It was a suitable place for a man who possessed a vigorous faith, a man who fully followed the Lord.

Mountains come in many different forms. Some are personal. All of us face personal mountains. The degree of difficulty may vary with our stage in life. Sometimes the twists and turns of living make it seem as if we are at the bottom of a steep hill. Day-to-day routines need not be exhausting. Steep grades do not have to overwhelm us. Personal mountains never have to stop us in our tracks. As Caleb found, following the Lord energizes us as we climb. Devotion to Christ empowers a believer regardless of the personal mountains to be faced.

In the pages that follow, I'm going to take you into the world of mountaineers. Using the rich imagery of climbing, you'll experience the thrill of reaching the summit, or what we climbers call "bagging" the mountain. These terms are a natural fit for the process of overcoming mythological mountains — those formidable barriers of culture, tradition, and practice that stand between us and our spiritual goals.

Few activities compare with the thrill of scaling physical mountains. Many mountaineers seek to achieve the goal of bagging the Seven Summits. The highest peaks on each of the seven continents include:

Australia's Kosciusko is only 7,316 feet high.
Antarctica's Vinson Massif stands 16,860 feet above sea level.
Europe's Elbrus towers at 18,481 feet.
Africa's Kilimanjaro looms at 19,340 feet.
North America's Mount McKinley soars at 20,320 feet.

South America's Aconcagua rises to 22,835 feet.

Asia's Everest is the granddaddy of them all measuring 29,035 feet.

Sir George Everest, a British military engineer, was the first to survey this glacier-covered peak in the Himalayas, which also serves as a Buddhist religious symbol. The Nepalese call Everest, *Sagarmatha*, meaning, "forehead in the sky." The people of Tibet christened the highest point in the world, *Chomolungma*, or "goddess, mother of the world." It is believed that Sir Edmund Hillary and Tenzing Norgay were the first men to conquer Everest, which is no small feat. More than 160 people have perished on her slopes from falling, smothering in avalanches, or being crushed by the massive frozen blocks of the Khumbu Icefall. Many succumb to the sub-zero temperatures familiar to the slopes and trails of Chomolungma.

Years ago, Sisley Huddleston told of a hiking trail near Mont Blanc, a mountain located in the French Alps.[3] This particular trail was a favorite of tourists because of its breathtaking scenery. Those who climbed to the top had the opportunity to see abundant wildlife and beautiful wildflowers that dotted the landscape. But it was an exceedingly difficult walk, some five miles one way. Even the most experienced hiker might spend the entire day getting in and out. In the late nineteenth century, someone had built a cabin a little over halfway up the mountain, a high-altitude way station for travelers to stop and take refreshment. A sign on the trail told hikers that they had arrived at the "Mediocris." The word is a compound Latin term *medius* (middle) and *ocris* (a rough stony mountain). Thus it means "the middle of the rugged mountain." Inside, weary travelers welcomed the relief this structure offered. They were greeted with something to drink and a hot meal. This respite also provided a beautiful view of the valley below. On cool days, which were many even in the summer, there would be a fire on the hearth.

Some pilgrims who cooled down, enjoyed nourishment and drank in the spectacular view were mesmerized to the point that they saw no need to finish the climb. The other hikers who persevered and made it to the top would return to tell their friends that no matter how pleasant the stay was in the chalet, it was nothing compared to the vista that awaited them at the end of the climb. Only those who pressed on beyond the "Mediocris" would experience that delight.

Many mountains we face are rooted in myths. Attitudes and actions that flow from myths touch most organizations, including the local church. Like the mountaineers who remained in the chalet Mediocris, many churches are locked into mythological thinking concerning issues related to church growth and wellness. Sadly, too many churches have chosen to go only halfway up the mountain. Think about the adjective "mediocre." It is defined as "of medium and unimpressive quality." A thesaurus amplifies this tepid word with no less than eighteen expressions including, *"average, fair, moderate, so-so, inferior, commonplace, ordinary, and unexceptional."*

In his book *Living Above the Level of Mediocrity*, Charles Swindoll challenges us to replace our bent toward low living by aspiring to excellence. He notes,

> Long enough have we taken our cues from those who ask, "Why be different?" or reason, "Let's do just enough to get by." Long enough have we settled for less than our best and convinced ourselves that quality and integrity and authenticity are negotiables. Call me a dreamer, but I'm convinced that achieving one's full potential is still a goal worth striving for — that excellence is still worth pursuing even if most yawn and a few sneer. And, yes, even if I should fail occasionally while reaching. Failure, remember, is not the crime.[4]

Granted, mediocrity is common to many things in life. It is measured in the attitudes of students in the classroom, seen in the activity of athletes in the heat of competition, and even expressed in the service one

receives in a restaurant. It may well portray a resting point for mountaineers in the French Alps. But if mediocrity describes one contemporary church, it is one too many! The question is, "Does mediocrity portray *your church*?" Does it characterize the members of your church? In
this day when a carton of milk seems to have a longer shelf life than
some church members, it's time to take a hard look at us. It's imperative that we reflect on the mythological mountains that may be hinder-
ing our effectiveness for Christ.

Left unchallenged, in time a myth will be perceived as authoritative and
normative. Soon that myth is adopted as a philosophy for living. Once
a woman was preparing a roast for her family mealtime. Taking a knife,
she cut the roast in two equal parts, and placed them in different pots.
When her husband asked, "Why do you do that?" she replied, "That's
the way my mother did it." Still wondering about the procedure, he
called his mother-in-law and asked, "Why do you cut a roast in two
pieces before you cook it?" He heard a similar response, "That's the way
my mother did it." Probing deeper he called the grandmother and
asked, "Why do you cut a roast in two pieces before you cook it?" She
replied, "I always cut the roast because I never owned a pot big enough
to cook the whole piece of meat!" When it comes to church membership, myths can create mountains that perpetuate limitations and even
spiritual bondage.

How desperately the church needs to hear the encouraging call, "We
can go all the way up the mountain." Remaining where we are as the
body of Christ comes at too high a cost. I believe it's time to claim high
ground for God's glory. It's time to grasp the heights. Rather than stop-
ping halfway up the mountain, let's set our sights on the summit and
begin the journey that will change us forever. How do we overtake
mountains in ministry? There are at least four attitudes for fellow hikers
to consider.

First, *be courageous while you persevere!*

As I have noted, Edmund Hillary and Tenzing Norgay were the first to courageously break the barrier and see the top of the world from the Everest summit. Since then many brave souls have climbed Everest. James Whittaker ascended via the South Col in 1963. Junko Tabei of Japan crawled and clawed her way to the top of "the goddess of the sky" in 1975. Amazingly, even a sixty-year-old climber named Lev Sarkisov conquered the summit in May of 1999. Mythological mountains in ministry are not easily overcome either! That is why a generation of dreamers, people with rare vision, need to step forward and climb with such intensity that it would make pioneer George Mallory proud.

Second, *constantly remind yourself of purpose!*

During an interview a reporter once asked Mallory, "Why do you want to climb Mount Everest?" His answer came quickly, "Because it's there!" Why should a pastor give himself to the grueling task of assaulting mythological mountains? Until these hills are conquered, they stand to hinder our effectiveness for Christ. Scripture clearly teaches that the purpose of the local church is to win the lost and disciple believers. Mythological mountains should be attacked and a victory celebration held on each summit. No longer will we allow ourselves to be nominal, mediocre Christians. We will achieve our purpose in His name!

Third, *make sure you are proactive not reactive!*

Climbing any of the Seven Summits is demanding. There is risk involved! But without risk there is little reward. Remember, attitude determines altitude! The best organizations are always renewing. They are always in process of initiating change, throwing out the worst, and retaining the best. Leith Anderson notes,

> When change occurs, there are many ways we can respond. But one thing is impossible: we cannot stay the same. We cannot stop the clock of change. If we choose to respond by doing nothing, change will take control and impose its will.[5]

Mythological mountains eventually make any church reactive rather than proactive. You ask, "Suppose we choose to remain where we are, so what?" While Thomas Hornbein ascended to the summit of Everest, reactive thoughts began to grasp his mind like a wolf attacking a helpless sheep. After weeks of climbing, he thought of quitting, of turning back. But then his attitude changed. His words haunt any of us who strive to conquer the mountains that hinder Christ's work. Hornbein noted,

> I looked down. Descent was totally unappetizing... . Too much labor, too many sleepless nights, too many dreams had been invested to bring us this far. We couldn't come back for another try next weekend. To go down now, even if we could have, would be descending to a future marked by one huge question: what might have been?[6]

Recognizing that we are involved in reactive ministry should disturb and alarm us! Instead of resigning to mediocrity, remaining halfway up the mountain, it is time to lace up our crampons and start climbing again.

Fourth, *develop an ever-deepening prayer life!*

Whether physical or mythological, climbing mountains can be discouraging work. We can lose perspective quickly. Upon assaulting and conquering the summit of Everest, Jon Krakauer, author of the best seller *Into Thin Air*, commented, "But now that I was finally here, standing on the summit of Mount Everest, I just couldn't summon the energy to care."

Communion with the Lord gives every believer necessary divine perspective. He keeps us caring when we climb. When doubts attack your heart, He energizes you to believe Him. Once the disciples Peter, James, and John came upon what seemed to be an impossible task. They could not heal a demon-possessed boy described as "one who often falls into the fire and often into the water." In a private moment following the encounter, this trio of followers inquired why they were unable to heal the boy. Matthew 17:20 records the stirring answer Jesus gave:

Because of the littleness of your faith; for truly I say to you, if you have faith as a mustard seed, you shall say to this mountain, "Move from here to there," and it shall move; and nothing shall be impossible to you.

Philosophical mountains built by years of mythological thinking have glared down upon the church for too long. It is time to believe the Lord for His best. There is no myth the Lord cannot conquer. I believe it is possible to take any mountain in Jesus' name. Years ago Caleb claimed his mountain. The contemporary church faces its own mountains — mythological, historical, or traditional. It's time to conquer them!

---

[1] Carl F. George, *Prepare Your Church for the Future* (Grand Rapids: Fleming H. Revell, 1992), 19.

[2] Alan Redpath, *Victorious Christian Living: Studies in the Book of Joshua* (Grand Rapids: Fleming H. Revell, 1955), 197-198.

[3] Sisley Huddleston, *France and the French* (London: Jonathan Cape Publishers, 1925).

[4] Charles R. Swindoll, *Living Above the Level of Mediocrity* (Waco: Word Books, 1987), 12-13.

[5] Leith Anderson, *Dying for Change* (Minneapolis: Bethany House, 1990), 139-140.

[6] Thomas F. Hornbein as quoted by Jon Krakauer, *Into Thin Air* (New York: Anchor Books, 1997), 207.

CHAPTER 2

We Have a Problem! — Mythological Mountains

If we take our Handbook seriously, we have to conclude that the church is the basic school of discipline and training for all Christians. And shouldn't our training be at least as serious as the military? After all, we are in warfare. None of us can have any illusions about that. And the battle is not just for flesh and blood; it is for eternal souls.[1]

For generations mariners lived by a code that restricted their voyages. What was that limiting factor? It was a common belief that the world was flat. No sailor in his right mind would throw caution to the wind by venturing to the earth's horizon. To do so would mean certain death because everyone knew that the world was flat. Enter a young Spaniard by the name of Christopher Columbus, who dreamed then dared in 1492 to sail beyond the accepted common belief. Sharing the importance of taking the "can't" out of our lives, motivational speaker Glenn Bland offers these compelling insights that illustrate the imprisoning snare called *myths*. Citing official documents, newspapers, and magazines widely read during their day, the "experts" believed:

- 1840 — "Anyone traveling at the speed of thirty miles per hour would surely suffocate."
- 1878 — "Electric lights are unworthy of serious attention."
- 1901 — "No possible combination can be united into a practical machine by which men shall fly."
- 1926 — (*from a scientist*) "The foolish idea of shooting at the moon is basically impossible."
- 1930 — (*another scientist*) "To harness the energy locked up in matter is impossible."[2]

Some commonly accepted beliefs are simply not true. We may believe they are and may even plan our lives accordingly. Take beliefs about the common cold. For years people thought that standing in the rain caused a person to catch a cold. If that is true, then why doesn't taking a shower make us sick? The fact remains that colds are the result of germs, not water droplets. Some people believe in good and bad luck, so they refuse to walk under ladders, dread the effects that come from breaking a mirror, and avoid black cats. These are the same people who comb patches of clover searching for the elusive four-leaf species. Once again, these notions, though widespread, are unsupported and untrue.

That is the nature of myths, which have a way of controlling people for generations. A dictionary in my study defines a *myth* as, "A traditional story presenting supernatural beings, ancestors, or heroes that serve as primordial types in a primitive view of the world." A myth is also, "Any fictitious or imaginary story, person, or thing."[3] Childhood stories from ancient Greece or mere mortals who execute legendary feats in the world of athletics are not my focus. Contemporary believers need to chew on these grainy words. A myth is:

A notion based more on tradition or convenience than on fact.

Bull's-eye! Sadly, even the body of Christ is not immune to mythological thinking. Mythological notions are limiting entire congregations throughout the world in their effectiveness for the Lord Jesus. What happens when a believer conveniently (or unintentionally) adopts a myth as a pattern for living? How do myths affect the local church?

First, *our past experiences define us!*

Remember that old Chinese proverb? "Insanity is doing what we have always done and expecting different results." Like a jet circling a runway, many churches remain in a holding pattern, because they have adopted the same mythological membership models that have been passed on from one generation to the next. And, true to form, we continue to see similar impact (or lack of it) on our world for Christ. Please don't misunderstand me. I *believe* in some traditions within the local church. With few exceptions, I hold a traditional view of the Christian faith. Jude 3 describes it as "the-once-and-for-all-delivered-unto-the-saints" kind of faith. I am a biblical inerrantist. I'm saved by grace, but I'm not mad about it! Biblical traditions are based upon the fact of God's Word. However, rather than being biblically based, some traditions in the local church are rooted in cultural thinking. Attitudes like:

- "Sunday morning services should be over by 12:00 noon!"
- "We must use hymnals when we sing!"
- "Guitars should not be played in the church!"

Pardon me, but at this point questions are crawling over my heart like ants on a Twinkie. Why should church be over by 12:00 noon? People who complain about the length of morning worship hours are often the folks who become euphoric when a ball game goes into overtime or extra innings! According to Ephesians 5:19, the early church sang hymns and spiritual songs, but did they use hymnals? Probably not. Some members become bent out of shape with the thought of someone playing a guitar inside a church. In 1818, while members of an Austrian church were preparing for their Christmas worship, the unthinkable happened! The church organ malfunctioned, leaving the congregation without an instrument to play. That's when Joseph Mohr penned the words of a now familiar hymn and then picked up his guitar and played:

Silent Night, holy night,
All is calm, all is bright,
Round yon virgin mother and child!
Holy Infant so tender and mild,
Sleep in heavenly peace,
Sleep in heavenly peace.

Thank you, Joseph Mohr. Celebrating Christmas without singing "Silent Night" is like celebrating the Fourth of July without firecrackers! Similarly, attitudes toward church membership are tainted with arguments that rise out of biblical silence. The fact is, some attitudes in a local church are based upon traditional tastes, not truth.

Second, *our present expectations confine us!*

A myth is to a church what a blue blanket is to Linus. Myths make us feel secure and safe. They help define tolerance points and comfort levels. A desire to move beyond mediocre ministry is met head-on by ingrained myths that whisper, "It's more convenient to remain halfway up the mountain."

As American civilization crept closer to western frontiers, St. Joseph, Missouri, was an intermediate point for travelers heading to the rich lands of California, Oregon, and Washington. As these settlers journeyed westward, a sign at the city limits haunted their decision. It read, "Choose your ruts carefully, for you will be in them for the next 1500 miles."

Like ruts are to the wheels of a Schooner wagon, myths are to a local church. Oftentimes, our myths predetermine how quickly our churches respond in the face of sorely needed ministry. Myths convince us that any attempt to get out of philosophical ruts will take too much energy. Years ago, I learned that ruts are nothing more than a grave with both ends kicked out. Left unchallenged, myths will keep any church in a rut.

One time, a friend and I took his beagles rabbit hunting. We placed these highly trained animals in a cage secured in the back of a truck, then we climbed into the cab and headed for a large, grassy field. As we drove for the next hour, all we could hear were the sounds of unhappy beagles. They growled and nipped at each other; they whimpered and whined. But when we reached our destination, a miraculous transformation occurred among the ranks of those canines. While one moment before, the dogs had been ready to chew each other up, suddenly the eager sound of high-pitched barking, muffled by underbrush and terrain, filled the air. Those beagles had a new priority — chasing rabbits! At that moment they were fulfilling their purpose. Born to hunt, they were in pursuit.

Do our attitudes toward church membership create a similar scenario? Are our expectations, or perhaps a lack of them, impacting what we do for Christ today? Are our myths creating chaos within the body of Christ? Do they feed thinking that fosters unproductive and damaging actions such as backbiting and criticism?

Like beagles released to hunt, the members in a local church can become productive, effective, and God-honoring if they are unleashed to do the work of ministry. Courageously dealing with myths will encourage members who remain halfway up the mountain to set their sights toward the summit, toward the loftier things of the Lord. Soon a myth that expresses itself with adages like "that's the way we've always done it" will be replaced with Caleb-like enthusiasm that says, "give me this mountain."

Third, *we are blind to our opportunities.*

Myths are vision stealers. They rob us of hope. When a myth captures the heart of a church, uncertainty plagues her members. Soon God's people miss open doors of opportunity to touch others in the name of the risen Lord Jesus. The early church faced mythological thinking head on. Gnosticism may have been framed from mythical legends that were folded into Old Testament history. For example, the Gnostics believed emanations extended from God to the creation. Such incipient heresy may be one reason why Paul twice warned Timothy to avoid myths. Some initial shots over the bow of this ship of heresy were fired when the mentor wrote,

> *As I urged you upon my departure for Macedonia, remain on at Ephesus, in order that you may instruct certain men not to teach strange doctrines, nor to pay attention to myths and endless genealogies, which give rise to mere speculation rather than furthering the administration of God which is by faith* (1 Timothy 1:3-4).

Was the Apostle content to end the discussion there? Many theologians believe the last words he penned comprise the second letter to Timothy, his son in the ministry. Was the focus pointed at his own needs? Had thirty years of toil and pain dulled the razor-sharp edge of his ministry? Had Paul resigned to remain halfway up the mountain? Read the penetrating words of a fellow hiker in 2 Timothy 4:3-4:

For the time will come when they will not endure sound doctrine; but wanting to have their ears tickled, they will accumulate for themselves teachers in accordance to their own desires; and will turn away their ears from the truth, and will turn aside to myths.

It has been said, "what one generation tolerates, the next grasps as truth." That's why Paul was adamant about Timothy *instructing certain men not to teach strange doctrines.* Like leaven is to bread, myths *give rise to mere speculation.* It is not long before evil speculations are sought out by immature believers who choose to think mythologically rather than biblically.

When it comes to church membership, have our churches adopted legends to guide them? Are they quick to listen to their myths and follow fiction at the expense of the Holy Writ? As one looks across the landscape of the local church, it seems that we are living in the last days. We have a problem! The problem is of such magnitude that we dare not delay taking bold steps to conquer it. It's time to redefine church membership! The myths that keep believers and leaders frozen in their tracks are spelled out in attitudes and ministry methodology. They are reflected in stagnant, unfruitful activity that does nothing to advance the kingdom of God. Just as world-class mountaineers bag the seven summits of the globe, we must conquer at least seven mythological mountains about church membership that are reflected in our churches:

Mythological Mountain # 1:	"The church is a volunteer organization."
Mythological Mountain # 2:	"We must manipulate members into ministry."
Mythological Mountain # 3:	"We cannot place expectations on church members."
Mythological Mountain # 4:	"Discipleship and evangelism are two separate issues."

Mythological Mountain # 5:	"Our programs take precedence over our purpose."
Mythological Mountain # 6:	"The eighty-twenty rule is the norm."
Mythological Mountain # 7:	"Belonging to a local church is not important."

Myths. Today, we fly in jetliners at speeds in excess of five hundred miles per hour. Electric lights are commonplace. Neil Armstrong, Alan Shepard, and a host of other Apollo astronauts would laugh at the notion that "this foolish idea of shooting at the moon is basically impossible." Albert Einstein would smile at the thought that it is impossible to harness the energy of an atom. Christopher Columbus would tell us there is life beyond the horizon. Stretch for it! Dream of it!

They said it could not be done. No way! Bringing a sixty-year-old naval vessel out of a graveyard in Crete, Greece, to Mobile, Alabama. It simply can't be done. But don't tell that to the twenty-nine crew members of an LST-325. The average age of these World War II and Korean War veterans was 72. Crossing the same waters that Columbus traveled some 500 years earlier, they completed a four-thousand-mile journey in less than four weeks.[4] Their story lives to remind us that you can teach old dogs new tricks. Another myth bites the dust!

I love the local church. It's out of that love that I plead that we take a close look at these mountains common to many congregations. My heart cries, "Lord, will we ever learn?" Let's lace up our boots and start walking forward. I think I see the first summit just ahead!

---

[1] Charles Colson, *The Body: Being Light in the Darkness* (Dallas: Word Publishing, 1992), 286.

[2] Glenn Bland, *Success: The Glenn Bland Method* (Wheaton: Tyndale House, 1972), 17.

[3] Peter Davies, *The American Heritage Dictionary of the English Language* (New York: Dell Publishing, 1972), 467.

[4] "Aging Vets Brave Atlantic and Old Ship," *The Virginian Pilot*, 6 Dec. 2000.

CHAPTER 3

Mythological Mountain #1: "The Church Is a Volunteer Organization"

O*ne of our greatest allies at present is the Church itself. Do not misunderstand me. I do not mean the Church as we see her spread out through all time and space and rooted in eternity, terrible as an army with banners. That, I confess, is a spectacle which makes our boldest tempters uneasy. But fortunately it is quite invisible to these humans.*[1]
[Excerpt from Screwtape's letter to Wormwood, both servants of the evil one.]

My roots are planted deeply in East Tennessee. Folks from

those rolling hills are clannish and, for the most part, conservative. We are rabid in our support of every sport played by the University of Tennessee, including ping-pong. Growing up, we were surprised to learn that "Rocky Top" was not the national anthem. Though I am not a spokesman for the Volunteer state, through the years I have grown weary of hearing three spurious claims:

- Yankees say that we don't know how to drive in snow. They will see the difference when NASCAR becomes a twelve-month sport!
- Other states advertise questionable food products as "barbecue." That is appalling to us.
- Folks on the western side of the Mississippi River imply that our mountains are too short.

It is not my desire to start a cold war, but the last claim is the most unreasonable. My first mountain expedition occurred in 1990. It was the day before Thanksgiving when two friends and I set out to climb Mount LeConte. Its peak is one of the highest in the Smoky Mountains. We chose to travel light that day for many reasons (or excuses). Each of our personal manifests included: a single 32-ounce bottle of water, one pound of trail mix, several pieces of fruit, three Snickers candy bars, one layer of clothes under our warm-ups, a cap, gloves, sunglasses, and tennis shoes!

Though there are several trails that lead hikers to the top of this ridge, we selected the most demanding and shortest route named The Alum Cave Trail. The round-trip journey was ten grueling miles. After about an hour, the elevation of the terrain became a steep challenge. We couldn't help but notice that the longer we climbed, the fewer people we encountered. Before long we began to experience dramatic changes in the temperature. The air temperature had dropped below 32 degrees Fahrenheit, and the water secreting from rocks froze, making the narrow dirt path extremely treacherous. At times the ice forced us to crawl to advance up the mountain. More bad news awaited us at the top.

Complimentary water, usually given to all hikers, was unavailable. The wind chill was sub-zero. We found an outcropping of rocks for temporary shelter, ate a quick snack, rested, and soaked in the breath-taking summit scene. From our vantage point we could see more than one hundred miles stretching across seven states!

The trip, however, was only half over. We had to descend before a rapidly setting sun left us without any light to finish our journey. Eight hours after our initial step onto the trail, we completed our hike. We were out of everything including food, water, and patience. My body screamed at me for days after this experience. This trip taught me several principles about hiking on mountains:

First, *when climbing a mountain, be prepared!*

I became a quick study on what I needed for such a day in the sun. Since then, I've been to the top of Mount LeConte several times and have enjoyed it immensely. One key is remembering the lessons from my first ascent. I carry enough water to shame a camel and enough food to feed a platoon.

Second, *when climbing a mountain, be focused!*

Each mountain demands a different set of abilities and thus different kinds of goals. For example, it is said that any fool can climb Everest. The trick is getting down from the top of the world! Focusing on priorities is a must. On one hike I severely injured myself by catching my toe on a root. Along with numerous scrapes and deep cuts, my ankle was severely twisted. I was forced to limp off the mountain. All this pain came because I lost focus.

Third, *when climbing a mountain, never go alone!*

When I first climbed Mount LeConte, I shared a moment with two friends that will last a lifetime. We fed on mutual encouragement. To this day, we share an accomplished goal.

The same principles are needed if we are to bag mythological mountains, too! One daunting peak for the local church is the notion *"the church is a volunteer organization."* Is this premise based on biblical truth? I believe this myth has been developed by narcissistic members! Beloved, we think too highly of ourselves. Charles Colson rattled the local church membership cage when he said,

> The roots of the church's identity crisis are found in the consumer mentality so pervasive in our culture.... most Americans are free to choose which church they will join or attend. And choose they do.
>
> Ask people what they look for in a church and the number one response is "fellowship." Other answers range from the "good sermons" to "the music program" to "youth activities for the kids" to "it makes me feel good." People flit about in search of what suits their taste at the moment.
>
> It's what some have called the "McChurch" mentality. Today it might be McDonald's for a Big Mac; tomorrow it's Wendy's salad bar; or perhaps the wonderful chicken sandwiches at Chick Fil-A. Thus, the church becomes just another retail outlet, faith just another commodity. People change congregations and preachers and even denominations as readily as they change banks or grocery stores.[2]

Amen, Chuck! It is a sad commentary, but the consumer mentality runs rampant in the local church. The average church member thinks that participation within a local church is strictly voluntary. Typical members stride in and out of the fellowship, as they desire. When it comes to supporting the work of ministry, rarely is giving sacrificial, and some give nothing at all. A member with the "McChurch" mindset thinks participation in service to Christ is based on what suits their fancy. It's no wonder why too often the church houses are full but the field of harvest remains virtually empty.

Consumer Christianity is now normative. The consumer Christian is one who utilizes the grace of God for forgiveness and the services of the church for special occasions, but does not give his or her life and innermost thoughts, feelings, and intentions over to the kingdom of heaven.[3]

For too long, church rolls have carried the weight of inactive and spiritually immature people who erroneously believe they may do as little as possible, yet remain a part of the local church. Records indicate that typically, on any given Sunday, an overwhelming percentage of church members is missing. Many of them have failed to darken the doors of a church in years. High opinions of ourselves have produced low living!

The task of bagging this mythological peak becomes pressing when we consider how God's Word describes the relationship of a local church and individual members. A definition of the church is in order here. The word "church" is translated from a compound Greek term of *ek* and *klesis* and it literally means "the called-out ones."

Years ago, W. A. Criswell, the fiery pastor of the famed First Baptist Church in Dallas, Texas, shed brilliant light upon this term when he wrote,

> For three hundred years after Christ what our Lord created was called the *ecclesia,* but when Constantine was converted and built those gorgeous temples they changed it from ecclesia to *kuriakos* — a lordly house. The same word moved through the languages: *kuriakos, kirkus, kirk, church.* But the Bible knows nothing about this, for the church of the Bible is an ecclesia, the called out people of the Lord.

Criswell continues,

> The church can be anywhere. It can be in a barn, it can gather on

a sawdust floor, it can be in a den or a cave, it can be in your house. The church can be anywhere, for the church is *you* [italics mine]; it is the people of the Lord, the called out people of God.[4]

Members of a local church, those who are rightly related to the Lord Jesus, are the called-out ones. Such an insight should cause the bar of expectation to automatically rise for becoming a member of a local church. Reminding believers in the early church of their spiritual history, the apostle Paul noted in Colossians 1:13,

> *For He delivered us from the domain of darkness, and transferred us to the kingdom of His beloved Son.*

An instantaneous transfer occurs in the spiritual world the moment anyone invites Jesus into his or her heart. Each believer is removed from the darkness and gloom of Satan's vile and controlling kingdom to the peaceful, reigning world of the Lord Jesus. Just as a fireman rushes into a burning house or a lifeguard dashes into the ocean for a drowning victim, each believer is *rescued!*

Elsewhere Paul raises our sights about being connected to the body of Christ when in sharp contrast to the temple of Aphrodite in Corinth where the priestesses were prostitutes, he proclaims,

> *Do you not know that… you are not your own? For you have been bought with a price: therefore glorify God in your body* (1 Corinthians 6:19-20).

What a compelling thought! We have been rescued from the tyranny of Satan by the blood of Jesus. His redeeming blood bought us out of sin's slave market. Truly, every believer has been bought with a price! The church is a voluntary organization? As Christ is in every believer, there is the Church. We didn't volunteer; we were called!

As we travel up the switchbacks of this mythological mountain, additional thoughts flood my mind. Although church is the usual description of those who belong to Christ, there are many other incredible biblical terms that vividly express the relationship existing between the Christ, Who is the Head, and the body, which is the church.

- *The Body of Christ* — Colossians 1:24
  ... I do my share on behalf of His body (which is the church) in filling up that which is lacking in Christ's afflictions.

- *The Bride of Christ* — Revelation 19:7
  Let us rejoice and be glad and give the glory to Him, for the marriage of the Lamb has come and His bride has made herself ready.

- *The House of Christ* — Hebrews 3:6
  But Christ was faithful as a Son over His house whose house we are, if we hold fast our confidence and the boast of our hope firm until the end.

- *The House of God* — Hebrews 10:21
  And since we have a great priest over the house of God ....

- *The Habitation of God* — Ephesians 2:19
  So then you are no longer strangers and aliens, but you are fellow citizens with the saints, and are of God's household ... .

- *The Temple of God* — 1 Corinthians 3:16
  Do you not know that you are a temple of God, and that the Spirit of God dwells in you?

- *God's Building* — 1 Corinthians 3:9
  For we are God's fellow workers; you are God's field, God's building.

- *A Spiritual House* — 1 Peter 2:5
  You also, as living stones, are being built up as a spiritual house for a holy priesthood, to offer up spiritual sacrifices acceptable to God through Jesus Christ.

- *The Light of the World* — Matthew 5:14
  You are the light of the world. A city set on a hill cannot be hidden.

- *The Salt of the Earth* — Matthew 5:13
  You are the salt of the earth; but if the salt has become tasteless, how will it be made salty again?

We may search the New Testament inside out and up and down and never find the narcissistic term "volunteer" to describe the church. The "what's in it for me" attitude has been allowed to slip into the minds and hearts of teachable people. Instead of calling people to live boldly for the Lord Jesus, they have been treated like impetuous consumers. Unless this mythological mountain is bagged, the "volunteer" mentality will intensify and shape the church of the future.

The loss of discipleship-building ministries in our churches can be underscored this way: "If you were to lead your neighbor to Christ today, in three years would you want that person to be like the average Christian?"[5]

Paul took his role in the body of Christ seriously and with responsibility. He used graphic imagery to describe his relationship to the local church. For example, in 2 Timothy 4:7, he likened himself to a soldier when he said, "I fought a good fight." His warm letter to Philemon begins with these words, "Paul a prisoner." Three times the Tarsus preacher called himself a "bond-servant." (Romans 1:1; Philippians 1:1; Titus 1:1). This term finds its roots in a Greek word that means "to bind." When Paul described himself as a "bond-servant," he made it clear that he was *called*, especially commissioned by Christ. In accepting his call, he took the position of slave to Christ with no rights or will of his own. He was to do always and only the will of his Master.

Consider these three powerful images: a soldier, a prisoner, and a slave. Like Paul, members of a local church are slaves for Christ, prisoners of His kingdom, and soldiers of His cross.

Not consumers, but soldiers of a conquering army of the Living God.
Not tourists, but prisoners under His divine authority.
Not volunteers, but slaves ready to do the bidding of their Master.

SETTING OUR SIGHTS FOR THE SUMMIT

We must seize a lofty view of church membership once again. Many steps are required to conquer a physical mountain. Conquering the mythological mountain that the church is a volunteer organization can happen, too. How?

First, *philosophy of ministry must square with Scripture — be prepared!*

Not much time has passed since a cereal company was reintroducing corn flakes to breakfast tables all over America by using the phrase "taste them again for the first time." Like those corn flakes, believers need a spiritual reintroduction to the biblical church. Take a Bible. Open it to the New Testament and begin reading again. Only this time invite the Holy Spirit to speak to your heart about service for the Lord Jesus through the local church. Ask Him to reveal agendas, biases, opinions, or behaviors in your life that are contrary to the clear teachings of His Word. Wherever He shows commitment waning, renew your heart to Him. If He uncovers unconfessed sin, do what it takes to remedy it. If a sour allegiance is revealed, change your mind to think of the local church as He does. Remember, Jesus "loved the church and gave Himself up for her" (Ephesians 5:25). Whether personal or churchwide, any philosophy of ministry that touches the local church but is not supported in Scripture needs to come under scrutiny and be modified to match the *ekklesia*.

Second, *rather than accepting things as they are — refocus!*

As long as we refuse to call people to lofty commitment to Jesus, they will be marginal for Christ and thereby marginal members. One reason the back door of a church remains wide open is that we place very low demands upon membership. We have been duped into thinking that a crowd is a church. Leaders of local churches may choose to float with the swelling currents of the times or stand against them. Focus on your congregation for a moment. Imagine each member being passionate about serving, giving, going, and living for Jesus. It will take time to transition your church to think of themselves as "called-out ones." In fact, it may take years. No church gets to wherever it is overnight. Earlier, I provided ten different images for the church. I could have easily given fifty. Pastor, that is six-months' worth of preaching material. Dig in! Study to show yourself approved. Use these expressions in your quiet time and ask the Lord to make your church *that kind of church*. Unless we make needed adjustments soon, Screwtape's words at the beginning of this chapter will become the norm. The nature of the Church will remain "quite invisible to these humans."

And finally, *overcoming entrenched opinions is tough — never go alone!*

Every time I climb Mount LeConte, I take encouragers along for the journey. The mythological mountain of the church as a volunteer organization can be overcome. We need to be a generation of pioneers willing to sink a flag of victory into her peak. As a believer, you are never alone. The Lord Jesus is with you every step of the journey and promises never to leave you or forsake you. If you are weary of climbing today, ask Him to encourage you. It is also true that all of us need "God with some flesh on." All of us need these champions in life. As I look back over the years, God has been faithful to provide wonderful people who came alongside me, at my invitation. Together we bagged a few hills and a mountain or two. Without them, life would have been lonely, and my ministry would have seemed desolate! But these people reminded me that God's hand was upon the adventure. Like the fingerprints of a child on a glass table, I have seen God's guiding hand through these fellow trekkers. If you are tempted to climb alone, don't. As you seek to overcome entrenched opinions, invite a few kindred spirits to join you. Who knows, they might be the people who help you keep your balance on top of the peak!

1 C. S. Lewis, *The Screwtape Letters* (Uhrichsville, Ohio: Barbour & Company, Inc., 1990), 15.

2 Charles Colson, *The Body*. 41.

3 Dallas Willard, *The Divine Conspiracy: Rediscovering Our Hidden Life in God* (San Francisco: Harper, 1998), 342.

4 W. A. Criswell, *Ephesians: An Exposition* (Grand Rapids: Zondervan Publishing, 1974), 105.

5 Gene Mims, *Kingdom Principles for Church Growth* (Nashville: LifeWay Press, 2001), 110.

CHAPTER 4

Mythological Mountain #2:
"We Must Manipulate
Members into Ministry."

M *inistry takes place when divine resources meet human needs through loving channels to the glory of God.*[1]

Mountain climbers who reach any summit, especially the summit called Everest, have a surge of intense elation. To beat the odds and attain a goal coveted for years triggers a sense of ecstasy beyond description. Such satisfaction also describes the feeling that comes to any minister of the gospel who catches sight of a mythological mountaintop, then dares to bag it. Fulfilling ministry is realized as God's people transition from the realm of mothballs to the reality of personal ministry within the local church. How do members make such a move? We have just stepped on the base of another mythological mountain in ministry. A visit to a local church is in order to better understand this philosophical ministry hill we are trying to capture.

Summer means Vacation Bible School for many children. On cue, the director of VBS invites participation of members when she pleads, "If you don't serve in VBS, then little children may go to hell." However, workers who give their time to VBS week often resemble Tom Hanks in the film *Castaway*. Anxiously awaiting rescue, they scratch their days of service into the gray walls of their minds. Others resemble the launch of a space shuttle as their mental clocks count down the remaining minutes of service. When the week is over, a collective sigh of relief can be heard throughout the halls of the local church.

It's the dog days of summer when a pastor stands in his pulpit to recruit members to serve in Sunday School for the next year. His heartfelt address is laced with arm-twisting, guilt-laden words like, "If you love Jesus, you will serve in our preschool ministry." Bubba Baptist stands in response saying, "Pastor, I love Jesus. Now honestly, I can't handle crying babies, but I will serve anyway."

Financial pressure and ministry go together like turkey and dressing. Many pastors feel they have to beg and plead for members to give through the church budget. Our churches are head over heels in debt, and many of them operate from week-to-week. Instead of being straightforward in those stress-filled moments, some pastors resort to subtlety. They say things like "If you don't tithe, God is going to get the money anyway."

Members are subjected to such manipulation routinely. As a result, a typical church member sees service for Christ as merely an annual event — working in Vacation Bible School or making a pledge to the budget

— not a lifestyle. They *tune out!* Because they are not excited about serving the Lord in a particular area of ministry, many believers *burn out!* Sacrifice that is based on unhealthy fear of the Lord causes a few to even *check out!* Like a splinter in your finger or a speck of dust in your eye, using guilt and manipultion as techniques to enlist workers in ministry is irritating.

During my college days, I was required to view the film *The Pike Syndrome*, which describes a type of behavior modication. A Northern pike was placed in a tank of water along with several minnows. One by one the Pike swallowed the tiny fish. Scientists added another feature to the experiment as they placed a clear barrier around the pike. Next, more minnows were introduced to the water on the other side of the glass. Seeing its favorite meal swimming around him, the pike went on the offense again. However, its attacks were met with painful resistance by the clear protective shield. After many unsuccessful attempts to eat the fish, the pike swam quietly in the water. When these scientists removed the barrier separating this aquatic food chain, something amazing occurred. Where once the minnows had been in peril of being eaten by a larger fish, now they could swim freely around the pike without fear. The pike *thought* it was unable to attack these fish, so it didn't.

If we could look inside the minds of many church members, we might see the same misconception tattooed on the walls of their skulls. Manipulative techniques meant to *encourage* service for the Lord Jesus have actually caused many members to be *discouraged*. Unless they are new Christians, every member has memories of serving in the local church. Negative history combined with hearing a leader's pleading verbal barrage is like adding water to a sugar cube. There will be meltdown!

A leader who does not recognize such a meltdown will continue this frustrating pattern unaware. Requests to serve in a local church are often questioned and then rejected unnecessarily by potential workers. As a result, a mythological mindset that says, "We must use manipulation to enlist workers" is fed. It is not long before such an attitude becomes mountainous. Years ago I learned,

> Sow a thought, reap an attitude.
> Sow an attitude, reap an action.
> Sow an action, reap a lifestyle.
> Sow a lifestyle, reap a destiny.

Our vision of church membership impacts what individual members become. Pastors, staff members, deacons, and leaders — listen carefully. If members are to be productive and fruitful for the Lord Jesus, then a radical change needs to occur within us — the church's leaders. Otherwise, our people may remain halfway up the mountain of ministry. They may be content living mediocre lives for the Savior. How can a church break this unproductive cycle? Is this mythological summit attainable? Does God's Word provide answers to this growing problem within the local church? Is it possible to involve believers in ministry that transforms them spiritually as well as those to whom they minister? We can answer all these questions with a resounding "Yes!"

The letter to the Ephesians is one of the Prison Epistles. It is believed that Paul, the missionary and Apostle, had been imprisoned in Rome near the barracks of the Praetorian Guard or possibly in rental quarters at his own expense for two years. During this time, he corresponded with believers who lived in this notable Asia Minor city. His powerful dispatch is an outstanding doctrinal treatise. The theme of Ephesians is God's eternal purpose to establish and complete His body, the church of Christ. A leader who applies the principles of this epistle to local church membership resembles a hiker who prepares for a summit ascent by attaching crampons to his boots. Let's step into some spiritual bindings and get a toehold as we climb this icy, mythological mountain.

Putting his pen to parchment, the Apostle highlights five spiritual gifts and then outlines why these gifts are given to the local church. In Ephesians 4:11-13 Paul says,

> *And He gave some as apostles, and some as prophets, and some as evangelists, and some as pastors and teachers, for the equipping of the saints for the work of service, to the building up of the body of Christ; until we all attain to the unity of the faith, and of the knowledge of the Son of God, to a mature man, to the measure of the stature which belongs to the fullness of Christ.*

Paul understood, "Sow a thought, reap an attitude. Sow an attitude, reap an action. Sow an action, reap a lifestyle. Sow a lifestyle, reap a destiny." Let's pause on the path toward our ascent and reach into the depths of these verses that wait to be retrieved like gold nuggets in the bottom of a stream. Bagging this mythological mountain demands answering a battery of basic questions.

Question # 1: *What are spiritual gifts?* "A spiritual gift is an expression of the Holy Spirit in the life of believers which empowers them to serve the body of Christ, the church."2 Salvation is *the gift of the Spirit.* According to Ephesians 1:13-14, everyone who establishes a relationship with Jesus Christ is sealed by His Spirit. Like earnest money is paid on the purchase of a house, the presence of the Spirit becomes the pledge of inheritance for every believer. His abiding presence is the down payment of our salvation. However, some confuse the *gift of the Spirit with gifts of the Spirit.* Including our text, spiritual gifts are listed in Romans 12, 1 Corinthians 12, and 1 Peter 4. "The one Holy Spirit who indwells the lives of all believers bestows many charismatic gifts. Each of them is a gift; none of them is *the* gift."[3] The compound Greek term *charismata* means "gift of grace," thus every believer is given at least one and often a mix of spiritual gifts.

Question # 2: *Who receives these gifts and why?* The nature of spiritual gifts indicates two truths. First, these grace gifts are given to believers, not unbelievers. Spiritual gifts are not talents, such as playing a piano or flute. Talents are developed by rote and practice rather than being Spirit endued. A "gifted" lost person may play an instrument beautifully, but that talent was developed, not supernaturally given. Spiritual gifts are given to believers exclusively. "Spiritual gifts pertain to the spiritual birth of Christians, not their natural birth. They are supernatural, but make use of and increase the natural abilities possessed."[4] Second, gifts of the Spirit equip believers for effective service. Paul said saints use their spiritual gifts "for the *katartismos* of the saints." Just as a doctor studies for years to perform delicate surgery to set broken bones, members are equipped to perform their gifts in the ministry of a local church. Interestingly, the same term is used to describe an important scene during the early days of our Lord's ministry. Matthew 4:18-21 records how Jesus, after praying all night, walked on the beautiful shores of Galilee. He called Peter and Andrew to follow Him. A few minutes later the Master saw James and John sitting in their father's boat *mending* their fishing nets. Every fisherman was expected to mend broken nets; otherwise, the nets would never fulfill their function. Like mending the strands of a fishnet, believers fulfill God's purpose in the local church as they are equipped to serve Him and His people.

Question # 3: *How might members be identified for ministry?* The local church is richly blessed with potential ministers because the Bible teaches that every saint is equipped "for the work of service." Michelangelo *attempted* forty-four statues in his lifetime, but he *finished* only fourteen of them. They are on display in museums today. Two of his masterpieces most familiar to many of us are sculptures of Moses and David. But the thirty unfinished pieces of art are interesting, too. They are huge chunks of marble from which the great artist sculpted only an elbow or wrist, or a leg with a foot and even toes, but the rest of the body remains locked in the marble. It will never come out! Unfinished statues are not the only masterpieces locked up. Many church members resemble these unfinished works of art. Ephesians 2:10 teaches that every saint is "His workmanship, created in Christ Jesus for good works, which God prepared beforehand, that we should walk in them." Instead of using manipulation to introduce members to life-changing ministry, we should create an environment that fosters growth, one that catches their imagination. It takes work to complete a masterpiece. And, it takes effort to develop people in ministry. There are no useless organs in the body of Christ. Each has some function. Everybody is somebody in Christ's body! Every born-again member of a local church is a master-piece in the making.

Question # 4: *Are there any signals of spiritual progress?* Several indicators will show spiritual progress. One result of members using their spiritual gifts is their personal service for Christ. Spiritual gifts in action produce spiritual development both within the member and in those they serve. Paul said there is "the building up of the body of Christ." Like a mountaineer sets a goal to climb a chosen peak, the goal of every member is to "attain the unity of the faith and of the knowl-edge of the Son of God." Spiritual progress is measured by spiritual maturity. The depth of a member's willingness to serve in the local church is a good indicator of the level of his or her spiritual maturity. Must guilt and manipulation be used to enlist workers into ministry? The great apostle might say to us, "Only if we want a church filled with mediocre believers."

SETTING OUR SIGHTS FOR THE SUMMIT

Has your limited view of ministry hindered God's people from climbing to the top of this daunting mountain? Any leader may engage members in ministry without placing them on a guilt-trip. Doing so means push-ing relentlessly for this summit. Be like Caleb and claim this peak for His glory. As we move into thin air, let's rely on some practical steps to help us keep our wits.

First, *instead of viewing ministry as a destination, consider it a jour-ney!*

There is tremendous joy in serving the Lord through His local church. Getting involved in the mainstream of humanity means ministry never ends. That's why we must engage people to continually invest their lives in the work of ministry. Oliver Cromwell was one of England's greatest political leaders. Once, when the British government began to run low on silver for coins, Cromwell sent his men into a local cathedral in search of the precious metal. After investigating the church, they reported, "The only silver we can find is in the statues of the saints standing in the corners." Cromwell, the soldier and statesman replied, "Good! We'll melt down the saints and put them in circulation."[5] Our myths about membership have allowed too many saints to remain safely out of circulation. Serving Jesus is a life-changing journey. (By the way, no one ever "arrives.")

Second, *teach people to serve the Lord with obedience!*

Samuel was the last judge of Israel as well as her first prophet. As a lad, Samuel attended to the needs of a priest by the name of Eli. One evening the Spirit of the Lord called to Samuel on two occasions. Thinking it was Eli's voice, the boy rushed to the side of his aging mentor. The spiritually sensitive priest realized God's presence and commanded Samuel to offer this response:

> *Go lie down, and it shall be if He calls you, that you shall say, "Speak, Lord, for Thy servant is listening." … Then the Lord came and stood and called as at other times, "Samuel! Samuel!" And Samuel said, "Speak, for Thy servant is listening"* (1 Samuel 3:9-10).

The second verse reveals the heart of obedience. Samuel was willing to listen. He was eager to hear with a view to obeying. Bagging this mythological mountain demands a similar response. Could the reason for a lack of involvement in the local church be the result of wholesale disobedience by members? If the body of Christ would hear and respond to God's call to service in Samuel-like obedience, the idea of using manipulation to enlist workers would pass away.

Third, *become a mentor and model.*

Professional mountain climbers who set their sights on the summit of Everest rarely go alone. Guides called Sherpas go with them every step of the way. Oftentimes, these experts tow their clients by "short-roping" them, a technique that attaches a small rope from the Sherpas to their partners. Short-roping makes the ascent safer and faster for the duo. Pastor, you alone cannot bag the mythological mountain of using guilt and manipulation to enlist workers. Nor will members move ahead of you. You must adopt the role of a mentor. Paul mentored Timothy when he said, "Kindle afresh the gift of God which is in you." God's people need similar encouragement. Become a model of spiritual gifts. Be transparent as you open yourself to new avenues of service for people and the Lord Jesus.

> Believers must be empowered to serve. Throughout His ministry Jesus empowered, equipped, discipled, trained, built up, developed, and prepared His disciples to serve. The Holy Spirit empowers the church to develop servant leaders who depend on His power. Believers use their spiritual gift(s) to equip others. For example, those who don't have the gift of mercy are still called to be merciful. The one best equipped to teach and train them about mercy is the one with that gift![6]

Fourth, *be a giver not a taker!*

Like reaching the summit of a lofty mountain, ministry is demanding. Ministry in a local church is where bottom-line theology is given top priority. It's where life translates into raw experience. Hard core ministry does not occur in theological ivory towers. It happens in the broken lives of people. That's why we must seek to serve our Lord in the basement rather than by the bay windows. In his book *Keeping Your Heart for Ministry,* Mike Miller relates:

I'm reminded about a story involving a young man in trouble and the response of his Quaker church family. The young man had stolen a car and had been caught red-handed. The elders of his church met, and the serious situation was presented by one of the men. Their immediate response was, "Where did we go wrong? How have we failed this boy, allowing him to get into this kind of trouble?" Their first thoughts were not of blame, criticism, or even punishment. Because they loved him and were concerned about him spiritually, they demonstrated compassion for him in his crisis.

When Jesus looked on the multitudes, He saw them lacking a shepherd. They needed someone to care for them, to guide them, to protect them. Today in your ministry, people are in the same condition. When you keep your heart for the world, you can reach out and minister to a helpless world with a heart of compassion.[7]

Do you know the story of Richard Hassell, a world-class mountain climber? A partial review of his extensive resumé is a mere glimpse of his greatness.

- Richard appeared in several classic Hollywood movies including *Gone With the Wind, The Ten Commandments*, and *Showboat*.
- He worked side by side with the likes of Gary Cooper and John Wayne.
- He was one of President Bush's "Thousand Points of Light."
- In 1989, he was nominated for the Nobel Peace Prize.
- His life was featured on NBC's Nightly News.
- The Virginia General Assembly recognized him.
- In 1999, the Norfolk City Council named a street in his honor.[8]

Mr. Hassell received several awards for his contributions to the Tidewater communities of Virginia. About ten years ago, the Urban League of Hampton Roads honored this servant with the prestigious "Vivian Carter Mason Meritorious Award." However, he failed to pick up the award. Instead, on his way to the banquet, he stopped to help victims of a house fire.

Richard's mother, Sophie Hassell, ran a soup kitchen during the Great Depression. Granting her dying request to carry on her work, this good Samaritan left the glitz of Hollywood to minister to the poor. He chose the basement, not the bay windows of life. This eighty-four-year-old man cared for the elderly, fed the hungry, and cried with the lonely. Richard Hassell based all his work from his modest apartment, traveled from need to need in a donated van, and funded his ministry with his social security check. He was a giver not a taker.

Illustrating the importance of service, Jesus washed the dirty feet of His disciples without apology. Imagine the Creator serving the creation! Like Richard Hassell, isn't it time for His creation to begin to serve Him? Neither guilt nor manipulation will ever move people into ministry. Realizing God's grace will!

---

[1] Warren Wiersbe, *On Being a Servant of God* (Grand Rapids: Baker Books, 1993), 3.

[2] C. Gene Wilkes, *Jesus On Leadership: Becoming a Servant Leader* (Nashville: LifeWay Press, 1996), 38.

[3] J. W. MacGorman, *The Gifts of the Spirit* (Nashville: Broadman Press, 1974), 30.

[4] J. Oswald Sanders, *The Holy Spirit and His Gifts* (Grand Rapids: Zondervan, 1940), 112.

[5] Charles R. Swindoll, *The Finishing Touch* (Dallas: Word, 1994), 256.

[6] Gene Mims, *Kingdom Principles for Church Growth* (Nashville: LifeWay Press, 2001), 112.

[7] Michael D. Miller, *Keeping Your Heart for Ministry* (Nashville: LifeWay Press, 2001), 109.

[8] Obituary of Richard Hassell, *The Virginian* Pilot, 23 Jan. 2001 plus additional articles on 25 Jan. and 26 Jan. 2001.

CHAPTER 5

Mythological Mountain #3:
"We Cannot Place Expectations on Church Members."

*M*ost church members live so far
below the standard, you'd have
to backslide to be in fellowship. We are so subnormal that if we were
to become normal, people would think we were abnormal![1]

Climbing a mountain — whether personal, physical, or mythological — is not for the faint of heart. Ascending summits of the
great mountains of the world is dangerous work. Sometimes we
hear of outstanding human achievements like mountaineer
Pete Athans, who holds the record as the only Westerner who
has reached the Everest summit six times. But there is also a

dark side of mountaineering. Writer and trekker Jon Krakauer, who ascended Everest in the late 1990's, offers an emotional glimpse into the hazards of this high altitude sport:

> At 21,000 feet, dizzy from the heat, I came upon a large object wrapped in blue plastic sheeting beside the trail. It took my altitude-impaired gray matter a minute or two to comprehend that the object was a human body. Shocked and disturbed, I stared at it for several minutes.[2]

Ascending Everest is no small feat; more than 160 people have perished in the attempt. This victim was a Sherpa who had died three years earlier. Two days later, while in an attempt to accelerate his acclimatization, Krakauer came upon another body in the snow. Actually, it was the lower half of a body. The clothing style and vintage leather boots were clues that the victim was European and that the corpse had lain on the mountain at least ten to as many as fifteen years! Krakauer's insights are profound as he relates:

> The first body had left me badly shaken for several hours; the shock of encountering the second wore off almost immediately. Few of the climbers trudging by had given either corpse more than a passing glance. It was as if there were an unspoken agreement on the mountain to pretend that these desiccated remains weren't real — as if none of us dared to acknowledge what was at stake here.[3]

Like a lioness who quietly waits in tall weeds to overtake her prey, the forces of nature are poised to snatch any weary, unsuspecting climber who plods up the slopes into thin air. One life-threatening danger to climbers is called High Altitude Pulmonary Edema, or HAPE. This mysterious illness is potentially lethal and is brought on by climbing too high, too fast. Such accelerated ascents result in the lungs filling up with fluid. The root of the problem is believed to be a lack of oxygen compounded by high pressure in the pulmonary arteries, causing the arteries to leak fluid into the lungs. Climbers succumbing to this high-altitude sickness will die unless there is rapid descent.

Just as a physical mountain affects a climber, there is a mythological mountain impacting the hearts and hampering the abilities of members in most every local church. The notion that says "you cannot place expectations on church members" is as deadly as any thinking in the contemporary church. Few churches ever experience high-altitude living for Jesus because they fear conquering their myths, especially the belief that placing expectations on members is taboo. Could this be one of the reasons why 70% of the churches in America have either plateaued or have begun a painful decline?

The absence of expectations on membership has allowed a mindset of mediocrity to determine the reach of effectiveness of too many churches. Rather than addressing the consequences of no expectations on members, mediocre churches are content to remain only halfway up the mountain. A plethora of examples show what occurs in a typical local church body that has little or no expectations of its members. At the onset, symptoms of HAPE are barely noticeable to the climber, but soon become apparent and life-threatening. A church, struggling in the grip of this myth, may fail to spot the enemy that threatens its very life. Let's examine difficulties in the realm of:

First, *personal passion: devoted commitment is diluted by apathy.*

No church ever remains stagnant. Like a physical body, every church is changing constantly. Like the seasons of a year, a healthy congregation will cycle between growth and dormancy. However, when a church ceases calling for the highest commitment from people, especially members, inevitably the devotion and commitment to the church is impacted negatively.

Did you know that water seeks the lowest level? Imagine a twelve-ounce container filled with only six ounces of water. Rather than collecting around the rim, water remains at the bottom of the container until an outside force changes the position of the container. Many people in the local church are like water. They run to the lowest levels of commitment. Left unchallenged and undisturbed, they will remain there.

A congregation that does not resist the myth that you cannot place expectations on its members reminds me of a letter that Jesus wrote. His strong words are recorded in Revelation 3:14-22. The people had lost their heart. They were no longer passionate about the things of God. They took on the characteristics of the river that flowed near their city. Like that water, these saints were neither cold nor hot. Jesus called them *lukewarm*. Fritz Rienecker noted,

> The contrast here is between the hot medicinal waters of Hierapolis and the cold, pure waters of Colossae. Thus, the church in Laodicea was providing neither refreshment for its spiritual weary nor healing for the spiritual sick. It was totally ineffective and thus distasteful to the Lord.[4]

A church that has low expectations of its members is a lukewarm church. Membership rolls of such a congregation overflow with people who remain undisturbed by their low living. They become quite comfortable in their indifference to spiritual matters. They are content with a *mediocre* life and faith.

Picking out people with no passion for Christ in the pew is easy. They are the last to give financially but the first to speak up in a business meeting that discusses how church money is spent. They will come to a fellowship meal but refuse a heartfelt call to prayer and fasting. They seek God's hand, not His face. Friday night football thrills them far more than Sunday morning Bible study. They complain if a church service goes past noon but rejoice when the playoffs go into overtime. But our

Lord would have the contemporary church to be boiling and repentant. Absent passion, members can simmer all their lives, never coming to a boil. Like the Laodiceans, they welcome the influences of this fallen world into their day-to-day living, all the while leaving the Savior on the outside, oblivious to His rightful audience. All this and more are the results of low expectancy by the body of Christ. Vance Havner called it "subnormal." Jesus called it sin and invites us to repentance. When a local church allows its people to seek the lowest spiritual levels, the coolness of apathy soon dilutes the fire of personal passion. Rather than mediocrity becoming the exception, it becomes the norm.

Second, *possibilities: the fervor of the church may lag!*

A church that is committed to calling its members to high-altitude living is rarely impacted by mediocrity. In fact, this body of believers will be fervent, exciting, and attractive to others. I do not know anyone who enjoys attending funeral services. Too many church services start at eleven o'clock sharp and end at twelve o'clock dull. "The clock struck at twelve at Sunday noon and the church gave up her dead."[5] Someone once said, "If you build a fire, people will come to watch it burn." That's true. Fires attract people. Recently, I was driving down a road and noticed black smoke billowing on the near horizon. Like a moth being drawn to light, my curiosity was spiked. As I drove closer to the flames, I began to weave through subdivisions and back streets in ways that would make Dallas Cowboys' running back Emmitt Smith proud. When I arrived at the scene, I joined several onlookers. There's just something compelling about a fire! If there is any place on the earth that should be fired up, it's a gathering of the church. People are just waiting to come to watch us burn for Jesus. Oh, that the fire of God would rest on His church!

Consider the fire in the Brooklyn Tabernacle Church. After reading Jim Cymbala's book, *Fresh Wind, Fresh Fire,* I was compelled to see the church at prayer firsthand. About a year ago, our staff and our spouses traveled to New York to attend the Brooklyn Tabernacle. But we did not focus on Sunday worship. We were not scouting out the facilities. We went to pray.

Finding Brooklyn Tabernacle Church is somewhat challenging unless you have a guide. Parking seemed to be non-existent. Our bus arrived one and one-half hours early for a prayer meeting that was to begin at 7:00 p.m. The worship center was 40% full when we walked into the auditorium to find a seat and wait for the appointed hour. We could not help but notice that the prayer meeting had already begun. The fervency of those present resembled a team warming up before a championship game. By the time 7:00 p.m. rolled around, the audience, which by now was overflowing, had kicked into overdrive. My spirit moved within me unlike anytime I have ever known. Moving from my seat to the altar, I was caught up in the thrill of spending time with God. One could sense intimacy, fervency, and power that come only from the presence of the Spirit of God! Two hours seemed like mere moments. During that time, I listened to people pray around me in no less than five different dialects. Hundreds of voices joined in unison to lift praises and requests to His throne. Testimonies to God's faithfulness and character were commonplace. While rejoicing through my tears, I began to wonder if the sounds I heard resembled anything like that prayer meeting in a Jerusalem Upper Room. God's people were meeting Jesus in this New York prayer closet. When the time came to leave, I was emotionally wiped out but spiritually charged. But this fertile experience was not over. I was overwhelmed with the fact that there was standing room only in the worship center. Every inch of space had a chair, and every seat was taken. A quick count of participants *in the foyer* exceeded 200 chairs, and all were occupied. This picture of fervency is the result of a body of believers who refused to remain halfway up the mountain.

Mediocrity in the local church is the result of low expectations. Bagging this mythological mountain means understanding something of lukewarm thinking and lukewarm living. Solomon provided insight into such apathy when he wrote:

I passed by the field of the sluggard,
And by the vineyard of the man lacking sense;
And behold, it was completely overgrown with thistles,
Its surface was covered with nettles,
And its stone wall was broken down.

When I saw, I reflected upon it;
I looked, and received instruction.
"A little sleep, a little slumber,
A little folding of the hands to rest,"
Then your poverty will come as a robber,
And your want like an armed man.

(Proverbs 24:30-34)

In ancient times, clearing land for a vineyard was a tremendous undertaking. Isaiah 5 points out the necessary steps that go into clearing and preparing the ground before a vineyard will produce grapes. Solomon reflected on a man who did not comprehend the possibilities surrounding him. He was lacking sense. Ground that was once purposed to provide a rich harvest now was overgrown and neglected. A stone wall used to keep cattle and sheep out of the vineyard lay broken in pieces. Solomon learned that people can be like that neglected vineyard.

A church may suffer under the tyranny of the myth that says, "you cannot place expectations on church members" without knowing it, just as no one knows when sleep finally comes. Sleep just happens! The moment we become complacent, we cease seeing possibilities in ministry. Left under-challenged, church members tend to become comfortable. Soon we forget what we have around us. We see obstacles, not opportunities. We forfeit climbing into thin air to find comfort in the well-worn chair of mediocrity. A church that adopts the myth "you cannot place expectations on church members" is doomed to suffer ill effects that are more damaging than the high altitude sickness of a mountaineer.

Third, *power: the church may become impotent.*

The human brain has what is called "a reticular activating system," a motivating brain function that goes into action during certain times in our lives. Otherwise, this system lies dormant inside our heads. For example, you may look into a full-length mirror every day. Then one morning you notice that fifteen pounds have been added to your waistline. At that moment you say, "I must lose this weight." The instant you set a goal to lose the weight, a particular thought process goes into action. Where once digging a grave with your teeth was second nature, you now count fat grams and calories. Shifts in your diet occur — salad replaces beef, and chocolate is no longer perceived as a food group. Exercise is added to your daily routine. When your reticular activating system goes into action, your mind helps you to see food differently. The specific goal of losing fifteen pounds turns on the reticular activating system. When tempted to eat dessert, you think differently and therefore refuse that fattening piece of cake.

Conference speaker and best-selling author Dr. John Maxwell is a perfect example of this process. He suffered a serious heart attack that almost cost him his life. During his recovery, his doctor placed him on a strict diet and daily exercise. One year later, as John and I enjoyed a meal together, he shared the changes that came as a result of setting a goal of becoming healthy again. John's low-fat diet included no refined sugar and no peanut butter. He also exercised without missing a single day. As a result, the John Maxwell of five years ago does not compare to the man we see today. One of the reasons for this transformation came the moment his reticular activating system was engaged. It made all the difference.

Myths cloud the thinking of a church. Doing God's business by our notions has become standard operating procedure in the average congregation. Thus, members are relegated to a particular mindset that hinders their effectiveness for the Lord Jesus. The strength of this congregation is weakened and true spiritual potential for these believers remains latent. Such is the case when a church believes that you cannot place expectations upon membership.

One contributing factor that allows the perpetuation of mythological thinking is "soulish Christians." Rather than seeking the mind of Christ with the eyes of faith, some churches operate by using their best thinking. Other congregations encourage members to experience a "feeling." There are those in church leadership who falsely believe that members need their emotions spiked regularly. They believe that motivating the dormant masses is the role and responsibility of the pastor and staff. It is then that the work of ministry falls into the realm of personal subjectivity. "This is what I think" and "this is how I feel," become spiritual barometers for local members rather than what God desires. In the end, the power of the church remains latent, untapped, and truly hidden, and its ministry impotent.

So how is power in a local church released? True spiritual power, the kind that transforms the vilest heart, is not born within anyone. Every believer in the Lord Jesus is introduced to His transforming power the moment Christ takes up residency in that person's repentant heart. The mythological mentality that believes "you cannot place expectations on church members" fails to recognize that once the Holy Spirit is unleashed through God's people, members rise to every expectation. Placing expectations on membership engages their spiritual reticular activating systems. They see the need, the resident Spirit urges them to meet responsibility and opportunity, and His power to make things happen propels their ministry.

Fourth, *people: the focus of the church is lost.*

Churches that choose to operate without placing expectations on its members have problems keeping their focus. Priorities of caring for and winning lost people are forgotten. Some churches are like the sign that was posted in a New York business. It read:

"Out of Business. Didn't Know What Our Business Was."

The same is true when 25% of Southern Baptist churches fail to report a single baptism in a year. These churches seem to be clueless as to what their business is. When only five percent of the members in a typical church consistently share their faith with lost people, we are virtually out of business. A church without expectations is impacted subtly at first. It's not long before members forget why they are there. Our business is to glorify the Lord. One way we bring Him highest praise is when our ministry focuses on the relentless pursuit of rescuing the perishing. A high-expectation church is one that keeps its focus clearly before members. Whether they have been there a month or twenty years, the members of First Baptist Church of Norfolk are continually challenged to focus on other people, to build relationships with them, and to minister to hurting folks of every kind in our community. Without focus, every church will be content to remain halfway up the mountain.

Fifth, *posture: the function of the church is labored.*

The hardest work in a church is work that does not work. It does not result in growing the body of Christ numerically, spiritually, in ministry, or in kingdom advancement. Haven't we all felt like we were going around in circles doing unproductive work?[6]

Just as high-altitude climbers often find it difficult to breathe, a church with low expectations will find the everyday work of ministry increasingly labored. Ministry becomes harder because members see it as unimportant. Whether it is corporate or personal, true, biblical *worship* is surrendered to personal biases and tastes. Before long, members begin serving their forms instead of the God of heaven.

64

The hand of God is evident everywhere we look. He is at work, drawing people to Himself, convicting people of sin, and using life circumstances to cause them to see their spiritual needs. Because this is true, the church has abundant opportunity to minister and countless ways to do it. As we love people through ministry, we join God in His activity of redemption.

Fellowship is also impacted. Without expectations, members may feel free to introduce pet agendas into the life of the church. Unbridled agendas will polarize a church. There are people who will "spiritualize" issues, calling those who agree with their position "right" and those who disagree as "wrong." The truth is no person should be allowed to seize the heart of any church. Like individual believers, every church belongs to Jesus. It's not "my" church; it's not "your" church; it's His church. He bought it with His own blood.

A church that does not place expectations on its membership is opening Pandora's box concerning the faith. *Discipleship* will be compromised. Members will remain unchallenged or under-challenged. Left to themselves, they will see no need for applying the disciplines of the faith. Like a chain, a church is only as strong as its weakest member. Unless they are taught *some things*, they will believe *anything!* We need the reminder that our beliefs impact our behavior. If we do not learn to walk with God, we will walk with the world! Mediocre expectations produce indifferent members!

Evangelism will be misunderstood. How many members have replaced "go and tell" thinking with a "come and see" mentality? Church membership should be evaluated by how often folks "go" rather than "come." Members without expectations often become demanding of the limited resources of any church. The consumer mentality that dominates American society has crept into the church. Instead of serving, members expect to be served. They seek programs to meet their needs, or those of their families, rather than seeking to meet the needs of others.

In his book *Kingdom Principles for Church Growth*, Gene Mims speaks to the "go and tell" issue in this way:

> Ministry and evangelism are linked to one another as firmly as discipleship and evangelism. This logical priority leads us to conclude that a person's spiritual needs are more important than his or her physical needs. Persons' physical needs are vitally important, but their relationship with the Lord is paramount.
>
> Persons are separated from God until they are redeemed by His grace in Christ. Ministry to these individuals needs to be accompanied by Christian witness and needs to focus on their salvation as the ultimate goal of Christian ministry.[7]

SETTING OUR SIGHTS FOR THE SUMMIT

The mythological, gale-swept summit that purports we cannot place expectations upon church members needs bagging, and soon. Developing an effective ministry demands that contemporary churches address the aversion to placing expectations on membership. The dean of the Billy Graham School of Evangelism at Southern Baptist Theological Seminary is Dr. Thom Rainer. His book *High Expectations* points out fourteen reasons why members remain in churches. A study of 287 churches concluded one of the secrets to their effectiveness was a class designed for new members. These classes existed at four basic levels:

- *Available.* The class is available for new or prospective members. No particular emphasis to attend is given.

- *Encouraged.* The class is not required, but new or prospective members are strongly encouraged to participate.

- *Expected*. Though attendance in this class is not mandatory for membership, an ethos exists in the church which makes joining otherwise difficult. New members who do not attend the membership class are the exception rather than the rule.

- *Required*. No one will be granted membership before completing the new member class.[8]

Rainer notes that "retention rates increase significantly from level two (encouraged) to level three (expected). Another sizable increase takes place at level four (required)."[9]

People rise to expectations. Where there are no expectations, commitment and devotion are questionable. Like water, membership void of a clear call to servanthood will settle to the lowest levels. Why call for such a change in how we do church? Because the need for immediate, even required, settings for member assimilation is imperative. Before you dismiss this approach as unworkable in your church, let's consider some forces at work that must necessarily impact the decision.

First, *nominal members will always struggle with devotion.*

Who avoids a call to commitment within the local church? New believers will not reject commitment! They are generally the most teachable people in the world. Their learning curve is saturated with spiritual wonder and enthusiasm long lost by many other members. They are excited to do anything for Jesus! Nor do committed members mind a call to higher levels of commitment. They gladly welcome help in completing the tasks of doing the work of ministry. The people I have observed who reject the call to high expectations are nominal members. These people will vote to hold a church back, while doing little to assist the church in moving forward. Nominal members love rocking the boat but loathe rowing it! The membership rolls of most churches are filled with names of people with spiritual patterns that are less than excellent for Jesus. Rarely, if ever, will they share their faith. They give to the work of ministry infrequently, go in His name begrudgingly, and serve based on whimsy, not commitment.

Nominal members remind me of Petty Officer Kevin Corr, a young sailor who was thought to be lost at sea. Some presumed he fell overboard; others believed he fell into the hands of mischief. After a mammoth two-day search conducted by eight Navy ships and 2000 crew members, Corr was found alive on his vessel . . . hiding. He was AWOL — absent without leave. Nominal members are like this confused sailor. Hiding behind their excuses, they support the notions that "we cannot place expectations on church members." The local church then must invest time, energy, and other limited resources to reclaim them from the mediocre ranks of inactive status. It's time for God's people to rise up and proclaim a new day in local church membership.

Second, *eclecticism may become the norm in membership.*

The day of understanding simple doctrines and church polity has been replaced with an eclectic and inclusive attitude. Thus, a congregation may have several veins of faith sitting on the same pew. Unless membership expectations are spelled out, tension found in theological issues may persist and even heighten. Ascending this mythological mountain is one means of protecting the ethos of the faith.

Third, *the torch of leadership is changing hands as we speak.*

It will not be long before the Boomer[10] generation has the reins of the church firmly in its grasp. Baby Boomers, ("Boomers"), born between 1946 and 1964, are one of the largest generations in American history, some 75 million strong. This concerns me greatly because our generation is not brand loyal to anything. We are a flighty and fickle group of people. Our parents developed values from the hardships associated with the Great Depression and World War II. When it comes to the local church, many Boomers are in debt up to their eyeballs and thus unwilling or unable to offer consistent financial support. The Builder[11] generation, born between 1901 and 1925, are characterized as problem-solvers with a strong work ethic, and a no-nonsense attitude. When the Builder-generation monies dry up, will the financial foundation of the local church crumble? Will building debts incurred today be the Achilles' heel of the church in ten or twenty years? Whether we like it or not, the torch of leadership comes with immense responsibility. Calling membership to highest expectations is one way of developing another generation of followers of Christ.

Fourth, *the results of low expectations are evident.*

Unless there are dramatic changes and course corrections, the church seems to be moving toward an impoverished state. This is why we must begin calling for highest commitments from members of our local churches. Low expectations for church membership are the recipe for mediocrity. The status quo is good for anyone who thinks the local church is effective enough as is. I don't believe that at all. I believe the best days are before us. The road to the next level is always uphill. It's time to ascend this lofty peak and stake a claim for the Lord Jesus. Like mountaineers who press on, we must be found faithful until we reach the top of this mythological mindset.

1 Vance Havner, *Pepper 'n' Salt* (Grand Rapids: Baker Book House, 1966), 9.

2 Jon Krakauer, *Into Thin Air* (New York: Anchor Books, 1997), 138.

3 Krakauer, 139.

4 Fritz Rienecker, *A Linguistic Key to the Greek New Testament* (Grand Rapids: Zondervan Publishing, 1980), 821.

5 Havner, 11.

6 Gene Mims, *Kingdom Principles for Church Growth* (Nashville: LifeWay Press, 2001), 90.

7 Mims, 53.

8 Thom. S. Rainer, *High Expectations* (Nashville: Broadman & Holman, 1999), 172.

9 Rainer, 172.

10 Paul C. Light, *Baby Boomers* (New York: W. W. Norton & Company, 1988).

11 Louis B. Hanks, *Vision, Variety, & Vitality: Teaching Today's Adult Generation* (Nashville: Convention Press, 1996).

CHAPTER 6

Mythological Mountain #4:
"Discipleship and Evangelism
Are Two Separate Issues."

U*nfortunately the church seems to be emphasizing its appeal to the physical senses. We bait the lost with fine music, beautiful architecture, splendid fellowship, sensational topics, racy discussion of current events, and movies. When they do attend our services, they often take one sniff at our bait and say, "Cheap!" and go straight back to the world where they can get what they call the real thing.*[1]

Many men of God are frustrated because of what they see in the church today. Generally speaking, we are not the mighty army we should be. Our churches are full of stony-ground hearers who are tares among the wheat, murmurers, complainers, quenchers of the Spirit, and wolves among the sheep. They look as if they are entering into the sheepfold by the door, but in truth they climb up some other way, and our sincere twentieth century evangelical methods are accommodating it![2]

Previously, we discovered how high-altitude climbers face physical perils as they ascend through the thin air to the summit of a mountain. One common risk is the High Altitude Pulmonary Edema, or HAPE, mentioned earlier. Another medical hazard is called High Altitude Cerebral Edema. HACE tends to be even more deadly than HAPE. It occurs when fluid leaks from oxygen-starved cerebral blood vessels, causing severe swelling of the brain. Like a rattlesnake in a dark room, HACE can strike with a vengeance. Pressure builds within the skull resulting in rapid deterioration of motor and mental skills. Mountaineers who suffer from HACE stumble around like a drunk. They lose the ability to speak or think clearly. Victims suffering from HACE have been known to sleep up to twenty-four hours. What's worse, the affected climber rarely recognizes these changes in his ability to function. Unless the hiker is evacuated to lower altitudes immediately, he will succumb to the silent bandit of coma and then fall prey to the icy grip of the Grim Reaper.

We approach the most formidable mythological peak facing the contemporary church. It is never easy bagging a notion held by members of a local church, but the rewards of a successful outcome far exceed every ounce of effort necessary to clear our thinking about this myth. It's time to bag this notion once and for all. The thinking surrounding this myth is based more on convenience and tradition than upon the fact of God's Word. Like a thin-air climber unaware of his deteriorating medical condition, the local church is suffering from an illness that may prove to be deadly. What is this silent mythological intruder? It is the notion that says, "discipleship and evangelism are two separate issues." Why has this misconception become so mountainous within the context of the local church? Step aside, catch your breath, and ponder these things with me.

We need the Lord to lead us to the zenith of understanding and action.

A few days ago, a series of quotes crossed my desk which illustrates the dilemma concerning this myth. It's called "Funny." See if you agree.

Funny how we set our clocks to arise at 4:00 am or 5:00 am to be at a job by 7:30, yet when Sunday comes we can't get to church by 11:00 am to praise the one who gave us the jobs!

Funny how we call God our Father and Jesus our brother but find it hard to introduce them to our family.

Funny how small our sins seem but how big "their" sins are.

Funny how we demand justice for others but expect mercy from God.

Funny how much difficulty some have learning the gospel well enough to tell others but how simple it is to explain the latest gossip about someone else.

Funny how we can't think of anything to say when we pray but don't have any difficulty thinking of talking about it to a friend.

Funny how we are so quick to take directions from a total stranger when we are lost but are hesitant to take God's direction for our lives.

Funny how so many church-goers sing "Standing on the Promises" but all they do is sit on the premises.

Funny how people want God to answer their prayers but refuse to listen to His counsel.

Funny how people think they are going to Heaven but think there is no Hell.

Funny how it is okay to blame God for evil and suffering in the world, but it is not necessary to thank Him for what is good and pleasant.

Funny how when something goes wrong, we cry, "Lord, why me?" but when something goes right, we think, "Hey, it must be me!"

Or wait . . . maybe all this isn't so "funny" after all.[3]

When I consider how this mythological mountain is impacting the local church, it makes me think:

> Funny how our programs may see hundreds of people "saved" but few baptized.
>
> Funny how we tightly pack a pew for disorganized evangelistic campaigns on a weekday but are able to lie down on the same pew on Sunday.
>
> Funny how we vacation overseas but find it too far to go on a mission trip.
>
> Funny how we will cross the ocean to share the gospel with a stranger but will not cross the street to share Christ with a neighbor.
>
> Funny how we may baptize hundreds, but the Sunday School doesn't grow.
>
> Funny how we focus on the church "front door" but neglect the "back door."
>
> Funny how contemporary evangelism stresses making decisions but not disciples.

Honestly, it's not funny when we realize the high spiritual stakes that are at risk. Bagging the myth that discipleship and evangelism are two separate issues begins by defining these familiar theological terms. What is "evangelism" and what is "discipleship"?

First, let's define evangelism. The noun *euangelion* occurs 76 times in the Greek New Testament. It means "good news." So evangelism is sharing the good news. What's so good about the good news? Even though man is a sinner by nature and by choice, God loves him. Paul summarized the good news in Romans 5:8 when he wrote:

> *But God demonstrates His own love toward us, in that while we were yet sinners, Christ died for us.*

"Demonstrates" derives from the term *sunistesin* and means "to bring together." God did not just flippantly say to sinners, "I love you." Because of the amazing love of the Master Designer, all the pieces of redemption were brought together. The sum total of all the acts of His incredible graciousness are found when Jesus, His unique Son, died on the cross. And the moment a repentant sinner sees this divine demonstration of love and places trust in the Savior, he finds forgiveness of personal sin and establishes an eternal relationship with the Lord. That is *euangelion*, the good news!

As a noun, *euangelion* necessarily implies "being." Jesus described "being" on a Galilean hillside when he taught,

> *You are the salt of the earth; but if the salt has become tasteless, how will it be made salty again? It is good for nothing anymore, except to be thrown out and trampled under foot by men. You are the light of the world. A city set on a hill cannot be hidden. Nor do men light a lamp, and put it under the peck-measure, but on the lampstand; and it gives light to all who are in the house. Let your light shine before men in such a way that they may see your good works, and glorify your Father who is in heaven* (Matthew 5:13-16).

Do you see any connections? Jesus said "you *are* salt; you *are* light." These verses speak of *being* something. Before refrigeration, salt was vital to everyday life. Salt has a preserving quality about it. It arrests the decay of meat and fish. The citizens of Smithfield, Virginia, are known for a delicacy called "cured hams." The meat is preserved by salt. Salt adds flavor to food. The presence of a few grains of sodium chloride (salt) can make or break the taste of a prepared dish. What does Jesus want us to know about simple table salt? There are people all around us who are decaying spiritually. They need the salt that comes only from a Christian life. Furthermore, salt makes you thirsty for water. Believers make people thirsty for the water of life.

Dying people also need light. Light has one purpose. It chases darkness away. It's been several years since I went night fishing, but I have memories I will never forget – the smell of a surrounding fog lifting off the lake water, the sounds of crickets and jar flies penetrating the evening's silence, and the sight of Coleman lanterns flickering against the dark background of night. If fear of being alone ever arrested my heart, all I needed to do was look for one of those lanterns. Every light meant someone was near. Light penetrates darkness. It gives hope for the hopeless. What is the point? There are folks all around us who are anxious to find a flicker of light to shine their way. They desperately want it and need it. Jesus identifies His followers as salt and light. He did not say, "do the salt thing." We simply *are* salt. Nor does He command us to manufacture light; we shine because we *are* light.

Likewise, the good news *is* the *euangelion*. Now, the verb form *euange-lizo* occurs 56 times in the New Testament and shows "the Holy Spirit is present, at work, in action, and in control."[4] He controls the message, the messenger, and those who receive this message. The action of evangelizing is carried on several tracks. Personal witnessing, crusades, preaching, teaching, drama, and music are a few ways of doing the work of evangelism. In short, evangelism is the work of spreading the fact of the good news. Before we continue digesting the myth that "discipleship and evangelism are two separate issues," let's determine a second definition. What is a "disciple"?

Gaining the exact meaning of any word in the Bible means taking several steps. We must first go back to the original texts such as the Greek, Hebrew, or Aramaic to find literal definitions and then see how that word is used in context. Applying these principles to the term "disciple," the first step speaks of *attitude*, and the second step demonstrates certain *actions*. Consider the attitude of a disciple. The Greek term *mathetes* derives from the word *manthano* and means "to learn." So, a disciple is a learner.

There are all kinds of learning. Public education is achieved by studying, taking tests, and mastering a subject. Life educates us, too! Some call it "the school of hard knocks." But biblical learners are to be a different breed, for they take what they know and put it into action. Jesus spoke of this manner of learning when He said, "Take My yoke upon you, and *learn* [italics mine] from Me" (Matthew 11:29). What happens within a believer who *learns* of Jesus? Simply stated, there is spiritual transformation evidenced through his lifestyle. It is to "acquire a custom or habit."[5] Though it is involved, being a disciple of Jesus is more than a life of acquiring information. It means that what we constantly learn from Jesus impacts how we act; what we believe determines how we behave. To put it another way, it's when the rubber of our faith hits the road of our lives. Christopher Adsit adds this insight:

> A disciple is a person-in-process who is eager to learn and apply the truths that Jesus Christ teaches him, which will result in ever-deepening commitments to a Christ-like lifestyle.[6]

Besides the original twelve, Jesus had many followers. On one occasion He called them to entrust more areas of their lives to Him, but they were offended and stopped the process of learning. John 6:66 says, "As a result of this many of His disciples withdrew, and were not walking with Him anymore." It happened then, and it happens today. It seems the rolls of local churches are filled with people who have stopped the process of learning of Jesus. These people may give lots of money, attend every time the doors are open, have learned the jargon of Zion well, even study their Bibles often, but they are not *disciples.* Why? Because sometime in the past these saints walked away from Jesus. The point where the process of the attitude and action of their learning ceased is easily detected. It occurred the moment they said, "No, Lord!" "I'm not giving that up." "I refuse to take this step of faith." "I'm tired of learning of You."

Doesn't it seem odd when local churches say they are dedicated to learning about their Master, but they are made up of members who really don't care to learn any more? The culprit is thinking that discipleship is a destination and not a journey. Some members *think* and *act* as if they have arrived or achieved something. In John 15, Jesus summarized the disciple's life as an abiding relationship. From the Greek term *meno*, abide means "to remain." Unlike those who "were not walking with Him anymore," a disciple remains with Jesus! Remember, a disciple is a person-in-process who is eager to learn and apply the truths that Jesus Christ teaches him, which will result is ever-deepening commitments to a Christ-like lifestyle.[7]

Discipleship, then, is the process by which we learn about Him and become like Him. No one can be around Jesus for any period of time and not be influenced by Him. The evidences of a person who remains with Jesus are easily seen.

First, *it is a life devoted to bearing fruit.*

Believers are to "bear fruit" (John 15:2, 4, 16) and "much fruit" (5, 8). Years ago, Andrew Murray provided these profound words,

> And what is fruit? Something that the branch bears, not for itself, but for its owner. It is something that is to be gathered, and taken away. The branch does indeed receive sap from the vine for its own life, by which it grows thicker and stronger. But, this supply for its own maintenance is entirely subordinate to its fulfillment of the purpose of its existence — bearing fruit.[8]

The one object God has in making us a branch is that the Lord Jesus may bring life to men through us. The first aim of every believer is to live in conscious awareness that Jesus desires to carry out His purpose in us.

Second, *it is a life devoted to intercession.*

Jesus said, "If you abide in Me, and My words abide in you, ask whatever you wish, and it shall be done for you." (John 15:7) This promise of answered prayer is one of many found in Scripture. Being around Jesus creates a desire to remain in constant communication with Him. There is nothing worse than taking a trip with family members who are not talking to one another. But disciples become prayer warriors eager to talk with Him. They know how to approach the throne of mercy. They pray out of conviction, not crisis.

Third, *it is a life devoted to love and obedience.*

"Just as the Father has loved Me, I have also loved you; abide in My love. If you keep My commandments, you will abide in My love … ." (John 15:9-10). A believer who passionately loves Jesus will do what He says without hesitation. Words void of appropriate actions are like clouds without rain — useless, deceiving. A healthy, joyful obedience to the Lord always flows from a love relationship with Him.

Fourth, *it is a life devoted to replication.*

Carefully read John 15:16. Focus on the words, "that you should go and bear fruit, and that your fruit should remain." Did Jesus indicate that the life of a devoted, ever-learning disciple produces additional abiding relationships, who in turn begin their journey of learning of Him? Dying people are hungry to digest the fruit that the heavenly Vine produces through the life of a disciple. Just as an apple or a peach carries seeds in its core, being a disciple includes an element of replication.

In Matthew 13, Jesus taught the parable of the Sower. The season to get seed into rich, fertile soil was upon a farmer. His indiscriminate method of sowing resulted in the kernels falling on four different kinds of soil.

One was hard soil (Matthew 13:4); another was rocky (13:5). A third soil type is called "thorny" in verse seven. The last soil Jesus called "good." When the Creator calls something "good," it's time to get out the highlighter and see why! The reason this terrain was superior to the others is that it "yielded a crop, some a hundredfold, some sixty, and some thirty" (13:8). Same seed but with different results!

> In Palestine during New Testament times, the average ratio of harvesting grain seeds to those that were planted is said to have been less than eight to one. Even a tenfold crop would have been well above average; and the yields of which Jesus speaks would be truly phenomenal.[9]

MacArthur continues,

> Not only does Jesus assure us that the true believers bear fruit but that they bear it in great abundance: one a hundredfold, some sixty, and some thirty. Those figures represent phenomenal yields of 10,000 percent, 6,000 percent, and 3,000 percent. Believers differ in fruitbearing because they differ in commitment to obedience, but all are profusely fruitful.[10]

How fruitful? Jesus taught the spiritual returns are similar in the life of an obedient, abiding follower, for the spiritual fruit resulting from an abiding relationship is unparalleled.

SETTING OUR SIGHTS FOR THE SUMMIT

If the explanations of "evangelism" and "discipleship" are proper and if members of local churches applied these axioms, hope would abound for spiritual hikers who desire to go all the way to the top of this mythological mountain. What happens in a church that believes "discipleship and evangelism are two separate issues"?

First, *some church members may be tempted to compartmentalize their faith.*

If discipleship and evangelism can be separated, it means that some people will *choose* which area they think fits them. They become one-dimensional Christians thinking, "I'm going to go deeper with Jesus" or "I want to grow spiritually." Their faith is merely theoretical. They focus on the *attitudes* of a learner of Jesus. They may memorize half of the Bible but ignore a world that is dying around them. These members talk the talk but fail to walk the walk. Their worship becomes perfunctory, their ministry obligatory. As these guardians of the truth live on cruise control, their *attitudes* become saturated with this mythological thinking. On the other hand, some one-dimensional members center their attention on the *actions* of a learner of Jesus. These people may be the first to go on churchwide visitation to share their faith with prospects. They are active, energetic, and spirited. Some of them are "a mile wide and an inch deep." Because they think a follower of Jesus only involves being active for Him, they pour their lives into church work. Tragically, many of these members experience burnout.

In both instances, members suffer from destination disease. Some think they will "arrive" by reaching a subjective state of spirituality, while others believe they have "arrived" the moment they win someone to Christ. This negatively impacts the local church because such one-dimensional thinking leads people to live in mediocrity with a distorted understanding of what life in Christ is all about.

Second, *members may view each other, not Christ, as the model for the church.*

If someone believes being a follower is merely attitudinal, then the folks they touch will follow a similar path. Truth will be on display but with little or no passion. However, if a member thinks a learner of Jesus is defined by his activities alone, his influence on others will be evident.

There will be lots of passion but little or no foundational truth. In fact, Paul described these kinds of people as being "carried about by every wind of doctrine" (Ephesians 4:14). Sometimes, both species of believers are perceived as "spiritual" by the rank and file membership who think "this spiritual destination" is unattainable by the average Christian. Believing they will never arrive, they are content to remain halfway up the mountain. Mediocrity has just come knocking again, and the hopeless myth is transferred to the lives of another generation.

Third, *concerted efforts by the congregation are compromised.*

Which will a church do first? Do we disciple or evangelize? Should we dedicate six months to encouraging the church to focus on the attitudes of a follower of Christ and then six months to the actions of a disciple? Perhaps these priorities should be reversed. That is one problem with the poorly planned evangelistic campaigns mentioned earlier. Our "decisions" are not becoming "disciples!" That is as tragic as a stillborn birth.

Local churches continue to struggle under this burdensome mythological thinking. It's time to attain the summit of this mountain. As we head to the top, let's consider these steps along the trail.

- *Focus on the "congregation" instead of the "crowd."*

Someone once said, "You cannot climb a ladder with your hands in your pockets." The same is also true when climbing mythological mountains. It demands work beyond our convenience and moving beyond our traditional comfort zones. Bagging this mountain demands a commitment to the ongoing work of discipling people. The life of Jesus is a prime example. Though He ministered to thousands, He poured His life into a few people. His model illustrates that reaching the masses is best accomplished by replicating desired behaviors in a few. Just as a mentor's goal is to influence influencers, a disciple's goal is to pour his life into others so they bear fruit that abides.

- *Prioritize on "being" before "doing."*

The human body and fruit trees have something in common. They reproduce when they are healthy. A healthy brain does not strain to reproduce brain cells. When a tree is healthy, it does not grunt to bear its fruit. Similarly, a disciple is a person whose intimacy with Jesus is so close that his customs and day-to-day habits reveal a transformed life. It is out of the transformed life that Christ alone produces His fruit. Therefore, when one prioritizes on "being" a disciple, attitudes and actions will include a passion for evangelism. This fits with Matthew 28:18-20 as Jesus commands us to go and "make disciples." The actions of transformational discipleship flow out of relationship to the Master.

- *Discover ways to encourage the connection.*

Divorce discipleship from evangelism, and vision is lost. Any attempt to separate the actions of a follower of Jesus from the spiritual attitudes they are to display fosters an atmosphere of disconnection. When this myth is conquered, larger portions of a ready harvest will be reaped for His glory. Followers of Jesus will reject the temptation to remain halfway up the mountain. Refusing a life of mediocrity will become the standard, not the exception. The connection is vital to the future. Evangelism is accomplished to the same degree that disciples spend time in an abiding relationship with Jesus. The piercing words of C. T. Studd call us to the great task of discipling, the kind that gets more people involved in the harvest. He said,

> Some wish to live within the sound
> Of church or Chapel bell;
> I want to run a Rescue Shop
> Within a yard of hell.[11]

Two thousand years ago, Jesus clearly revealed that the objective of the local church is to make disciples. He understood that form follows function. Otherwise, all our church activity can be lost in aimlessness and confusion. Yes, He had a plan to win, and that plan involved investing massive amounts of time into a few men. Peter and John were two of the twelve. Their lives are prime examples of how discipleship and evangelism fit together like a hand in a glove. Luke the historian records that after Pentecost, these two men stood in the semi-circle of the Sanhedrin to give an account for preaching the good news.

> *Now as they observed the confidence of Peter and John, and understood that they were uneducated and untrained men, they were marveling, and began to recognize them as having been with Jesus* (Acts 4:13).

The plan is profoundly simple. Disciples of Jesus bear fruit, and it is natural, not forced. Like Peter and John, being with Jesus will always astound and be the envy of a watching world.

---

[1] Roy J. Fish and J. E. Conant, *Every Member Evangelism For Today* (New York: Harper & Row, 1976), 57.

[2] Ray Comfort, *Hell's Best Kept Secret* (Springdale, PA: Whitaker House, 1989), 45.

[3] Source Unknown

[4] David Barrett, *Evangelize! A Historical Survey of the Concept* (Birmingham: New Hope, 1987), 12.

[5] Harold K. Moulton, ed., *The Analytical Greek Lexicon Revised* (Grand Rapids: Zondervan, 1978), 257.

[6] Christopher B. Adsit, *Personal Disciplemaking* (Nashville: Thomas Nelson, 1993), 35.

[7] Adsit, 35.

[8] Andrew Murray, *The True Vine* (Springdale, PA: Whitaker House, 1982), 19.

[9] John MacArthur, *The MacArthur New Testament Commentary: Matthew 8-15* (Chicago: Moody, 1987), 346-7.

[10] MacArthur, 362.

[11] Norman P. Grubb, *C. T. Studd: Cricketer and Pioneer* (Philadelphia: Christian Literature Crusade, 1948), 66.

CHAPTER 7

Mythological Mountain #5:
"Our Programs Take Precedence Over Our Purpose."

*M*ost of the evangelistic efforts of the church begin with the multitudes under the assumption that the church is qualified to conserve what good is done. The result is our spectacular emphasis upon numbers of converts, candidates for baptism, and more members for the church, with little or no genuine concern manifested toward the establishment of these souls in the love and power of God, let alone the preservation and continuation of the work.

Surely if the pattern of Jesus at this point means anything at all it teaches that the first duty of a pastor as well as the first concern of an evangelist is to see to it that a foundation is laid in the beginning upon which can be built an effective and continuing evangelistic ministry to the multitudes. This will require more concentration of time and talents upon fewer men in the church while not neglecting the passion for the world. It will mean raising up trained leadership "for the work of ministering" with the pastor (Ephesians 4:12). A few people so dedicated in time will shake the world for God. Victory is never won by the multitudes.[1]

John Maxwell tells of a group of people who,

> were preparing for an ascent to the top of Mont Blanc in France in the Alps. On the evening before the climb, a French guide outlined the main prerequisite for success. He said, "To reach the top, you must carry only equipment necessary for climbing. You must leave behind all unnecessary accessories. It's a difficult climb."
>
> A young Englishman disagreed and the next morning showed up with a rather heavy, brightly colored blanket, some large pieces of cheese, a bottle of wine, a couple of cameras with several lenses hanging around his neck, and some bars of chocolate. The guide said, "You'll never make it with that. You can only take the bare necessities to make the climb."
>
> But strong-willed as he was, the Englishman set off on his own in front of the group to prove to them he could do it. The group then followed under the direction of the guide, each one carrying just the bare necessities. On the way up to the summit of Mont Blanc, they began to notice certain things someone had left along the way. First, they encountered a brightly colored blanket, then some pieces of cheese, a bottle of wine, camera equipment, and some chocolate bars. Finally, when they reached the top, they discovered the Englishman. Wisely along the way he had jettisoned everything unnecessary.[2]

Many local churches and the way they do ministry remind me of that Englishman. They are carrying too much baggage for the journey. For years, *The Ed Sullivan Show* was a popular variety television program. Any entertainer with ambitions of making it in show business knew that success often hinged on a single appearance on this famous program.

One memorable performer who impressed me was appropriately called "the plate spinner." Appearing before a live audience, he would take plates and one-by-one begin to spin them on the tops of sticks. The count of spinning plates climbed into the teens before losing their speed, falling off, and breaking on the stage floor. That scene aptly describes what occurs within the life of many local churches. They are attempting to spin too many ministry plates. "For many, Christianity has come to be just another activity, rather than a pervasive lifestyle characterized by a single-minded purpose to follow the Lord of life and harvest, laying all else aside."[3]

On the horizon stands another mythological mountain responsible for demoralizing more members than any other notion the contemporary church will face. It sneers at us, "Our programs take precedence over our purpose." The effects of such a mediocre outlook have pushed believers from a balanced, biblical approach in ministry to heart-pounding extremes. As a result, today many churches have long since forgotten why they exist.

Some churches who buy into this notion are finding it increasingly difficult to remain effective. Instead of excelling for Christ, they are barely keeping their heads above water. Instead of swimming, they are treading water. Instead of climbing to greater heights, they are content to remain halfway up the mountain.

Two lovable characters in *Winnie-the-Pooh* illustrate the merry-go-round on which some churches find themselves trapped. Let's pick up mid-story to see if we may identify this mythological thinking.

One fine winter's day when Piglet was brushing away the snow in front of his house, he happened to look up, and there was Winnie-the-Pooh. Pooh was walking round and round in a circle, thinking of someone else, and when Piglet called to him, he just went on walking.

> "Hallo!" said Piglet, "what are *you* doing?"
> "Hunting," said Pooh
> "Hunting what?" said Piglet, coming closer.
> "That's just what I ask myself. I ask myself, What?"
> "What do you think you'll answer?"
> "I shall have to wait until I catch up with it," said
> Winnie-the-Pooh.[4]

Now Pooh and Piglet continued their search together by walking around in a circle until they become enamored with their own tracks. They are convinced that the creatures they track are increasing in number and perhaps are even dangerous. Finally, Christopher Robin, sitting in a tree above them, sees their folly and gently corrects them.

> 'Silly old Bear,' he said, 'What *were* you doing? First you went around the spinney tree twice by yourself, and then Piglet ran after you and you went around again together, and then you were just going round a fourth time.'[5]

Does this adventure describe any churches you know? Does it peg *your* church? Many believers are locked into local churches that continually go around in circles. Unproductive and repetitious ministry results when we allow our fear of what lies ahead to overwhelm our faith in an omnipresent, omnipotent God. Our purpose becomes lost in the maze of endless and pointless ministry. Vision for changing the focus within the church and ideation for expanding ministry become as rare as a PETA[6] representative at a National Rifle Association rally. A congregation captured by this myth will bury a good idea in a variety of ways.

Here are six for starters,

- "It will never work."
- "We can't afford it."
- "We've never done it that way before."
- "We're not ready for it."
- "It's not our responsibility."
- "We're doing fine without it."

If needed, there are a half dozen excuses to use by any church looking for ways to remain mediocre. Instead of finding reasons to encourage effectiveness, we invest time, energy, efforts, and precious resources to support why we can't do something fresh in the King's name. Because we do not know where we are going, it is more *convenient* to remain where we are. Churches that allow programs to dictate their direction have these characteristics:

First, *they maintain. Rather than build synergy, programs may become a drain.*

Many church members have lots of energy, but a church that does not focus that energy surrenders the opportunity to be a force in the community. It does not have synergy. A church can be busy seven days a week, but activity does not guarantee productivity. It is the difference between a flashlight and a laser. A flashlight casts a harmless but broad beam of light across a specific area. This kind of light is limited in its usefulness. However, a laser is light concentrated. The beam from a laser is so strong that it can cut through metal, yet so focused that it may be used to perform delicate eye surgery.

If you go to the circus, watch when animal trainers enter a lion cage. They are armed with a whip and a pistol. But the most important tool the trainer uses is a stool. He holds the stool by the back and thrusts the legs toward the face of these dangerous cats. Attempting to focus on all the chair legs at one time mesmerizes the lions, who then become weak, tame, and disabled. Paralysis comes because their attention is fragmented.

The danger is that members of program-centered churches can suffer from similar fragmentation. Program-centered churches can tend to foster "a maintenance-mindset" within people, who over time become mesmerized with activity and helpless as a kitten.

Second, *they shift. Instead of developing people, programs may mishandle them.*

Several years ago while serving a church in East Tennessee, a deacon and I were discussing church work. He shared his struggle with resentment toward his father who "always chose to be at the church instead of spending time with me." In the same way, programs sometimes misuse people. A church that adopts the myth that "programs take precedence over purpose" tends to see people as expendable. Their programs become more valuable than the people who help perpetuate them. All of us need this gentle reminder that says, "love people and use things." When program-centered churches shift the priorities, they love the program and will use people to keep it running. Then, programs misuse people instead of developing them. This myth yields a harvest of barren regrets.

Third, *they value tradition. Because tradition carries influence, programs cost more than they produce.*

It is easy to see if a church allows programs to take precedence over purpose. Just look at the planning calendar for the next twelve months. There are churches that decide on their programs like the NCAA Basketball Tournament selects some basketball teams. Some are "automatic." That means programs move from one calendar to the next without any resistance or evaluation. It matters not if programs are ineffective because "that's the way we've always done it." Whether it's a youth choir tour or Vacation Bible School or an annual mission trip, left unchallenged, traditions will influence the calendar of a local church. Soon the value of the ministry is based on history rather than effectiveness. It is not long before these programs cost far more than they produce. In the marketplace they call that bankruptcy. In professional athletics it's called a waiver. In the local church it's business as usual.

Fourth, *they personalize. If a program diminishes, members feel shame and blame.*

If the results of a program decrease, the people supporting the effort suffer the embarrassment that comes with failure. They "own" the loss of this ministry. The collapse becomes their fault. "Apparently, they didn't work hard enough." "They are simply not committed!" After assassinating President Lincoln, John Wilkes Booth broke his leg when he jumped from the balcony of the Ford Theatre. A few miles later he was in a Virginia barn being attended to by Dr. Samuel Mudd. Not realizing that his patient was a criminal, Dr. Mudd set Booth's broken bone. As a result, the physician was accused of a crime and sentenced to prison. Thus, the belittling phrase is used, "His name is mud." Whenever a program collapses, some churches heap guilt and blame on the good people who faithfully served. Their name is mud.

Fifth, *they drive. Though it is not always apparent, some programs hide agendas.*

Many people attend church and serve in ministry for right reasons. They genuinely care for people and for the work that ministry does. But some people drive a church through a "pet" program. They financially support local church ministry as long as that program exists. Their attitude and attendance have the same prerequisites. Their loyalty to a particular ministry creates spiritual blinders for other work that may be essential for ministry. They guard church calendar time and budget line items that support the pet programs like a mother hen guards her chicks. As a result, unless it comes under needed evaluation, this "sacred cow" will sometimes drive the entire ministry of a local church.

SETTING OUR SIGHTS FOR THE SUMMIT

If the "our programs take precedence over our purpose" myth has captured the heart of your church, there is a solution. Just as there are multiple ways to ascend Mount Everest, there are several ways to climb this particular mythological mountain. The dreams of a spiritual summit push need not be abandoned nor left halfway up the mountain. We can climb. We can bag this notion. We can stand victoriously on the top of this crest. To do so begins with a clearly defined purpose. Every local church needs a regular reminder of why it exists. When that occurs, "pet programs" will take a welcomed hike! Assuring that this myth does not grip the heart of a local church demands a process that identifies "why we exist" as well as the steps to implement that stated purpose. What steps might be necessary in that process?

Step # 1: *Develop a ministry-wide baseline.*

Every effective strategy begins with a baseline. You need to know where you are. The difference between *perceived* reality and reality are as opposite as the poles on a magnet. One is subjective; the other is objective. *Perceived* reality hides agendas whereas reality reveals them. The aim for leaders in a local church is to create a concerted ministry effort. This means no program is allowed to spin on its own axis. Each program is evaluated on how it contributes to the church's clearly defined purpose.

Becoming accountable to the church, not the individuals who drive the program, is the key here. Years ago, some wag said, "An effective pastor needs the heart of a mother, the eyes of an eagle, the strength of a Samson, and the skin of a rhinoceros." Developing ministry baselines should not become an attack on people, including the pastor, deacons, and members. It is simply discovering where you are. People who do not know where they are, are considered lost. Some churches are like that, lost as a ball in tall weeds! Discovering a baseline helps us find where we are in ministry. Without this step, analysis of ministry will be incorrect and planning will suffer. In the end, the local church may be content to remain halfway up the mountain.

We took this initial step several years ago when I became pastor of First Baptist Church of Norfolk. Almost two hundred leaders were asked to help me discover our location. "Where are we?" was the question posed to this group. After weeks of discovery, we found out!

Step # 2: *Write a clearly defined purpose statement.*

The reason the mindset "our programs take precedence over our purpose" exists is due in part to the fact that:

- A church does not have a written purpose statement.
- A written purpose statement is not applied correctly.
- A written purpose statement is unacceptable to the church.

All three mistakes must be avoided if we are to bag this mythological mountain. Why does a church need a clearly defined purpose? If you do not know where you are going, you will not know when you arrive, nor will you like it when you get there.

The process of writing a purpose statement begins with an open Bible. Matthew 18:11 and Luke 19:10 preserve the reason why Jesus came from heaven to this earth.

For the Son of Man has come to seek and to save that which was lost.

I do not believe Jesus spoke an idle word or wasted one second of His sacred life. Each day He fulfilled the Father's divine purpose by searching out hurting, hell-bound people and offering His forgiveness. That remains His purpose today! And so there would be no misunderstanding about His purpose for His church, Jesus restated the Great Commission throughout the Gospels and Acts (Matthew 28:18-20, Mark 16:15-16, Luke 24:47-48, Acts 1:8). The Apostle Paul hinted for the church to keep on purpose when he said,

> *Therefore be careful how you walk, not as unwise men, but as wise, making the most of your time, because the days are evil* (Ephesians 5:15-16).

After thoroughly studying the Great Commission passages, the leadership team I mentioned embarked on writing a purpose statement for our church. It says,

> The First Baptist Church of Norfolk exists to glorify God by winning all the people of our community and leading them to become fully devoted followers of Jesus Christ.

Our statement flows from God's Word. It's clear enough that even our children publicly rehearsed it during the Wednesday evening meals. This purpose statement was approved unanimously by our church and is our benchmark for evaluating ministry. Our people understand that the purpose statement defines the playing field and everything else is out of bounds. Here are some advantages that come from operating ministry through a clearly defined purpose statement.

- It sets boundaries in ministry.
- It allows us the opportunity to say, "Thanks, but no thanks."
- It addresses "agendas" positively.
- It puts us in a proactive position rather than a reactive one.

Nothing encourages a discouraged church faster than to discover or rediscover why it exists. Without a well-written statement of purpose a church may be like Winnie-the-Pooh. We focus on the wrong things and end up going around in circles. Our purpose will keep us climbing to the top of the mountain.

Step # 3: *Spell out your church's "values."*

A purpose statement reminds us of why we exist. But every church also needs well-defined core values. These values assist the congregation in determining what is important. They outline the functions of a church. The work of our church has been categorized into six functions: worship, discipleship, evangelism, fellowship, relationships, and ministry. A church needs to focus on what it values. God's people should prize what is valuable. If it is not important, a congregation should not do it. The membership of First Baptist Church of Norfolk has adopted the following core values:

- Exalting: We seek intimate fellowship with God.
- Equipping: We equip our fellowship to practice the faith.
- Evangelizing: We passionately share the gospel.
- Encouraging: We encourage one another to grow in faith and service.
- Edifying: We strengthen one another through caring relationships.
- Exemplifying: We expect every member to join us in ministry.

The importance of "church wellness" cannot be underestimated. That's where core values help by creating a systemic approach in ministry planning and productivity.

Step # 4: *Formulate your objectives.*

What does your church desire to accomplish? If is it to merely increase nickels and noses, you miss the point. The best advertising for a church is changed lives. Like an automobile has a prototype, a church needs to design ministry with the objective of assisting people in becoming more and more like Jesus. Objectives should be broad enough to keep people dreaming, yet focused enough to keep them climbing. Some identify this process as a long-range plan. But objectives also lead a wise church in writing specific goals. Objectives help any local church to discover its uniqueness in the kingdom. Objectives keep a congregation from yielding to the temptation of being "the eighth lemonade stand in a row of ten."

Step # 5: *Write specific goals.*

Goals and plans are the magic keys to happiness and success. Only 3 percent of all people have goals and plans and write them down. Ten percent more have goals and plans, but keep them in their heads. The rest — 87 percent — drift through life without definite goals or plans. They do not know where they are going and others dictate to them.[7]

After discovering our baseline and writing a purpose statement and objectives, the next step was writing the strategic ministry plan of First Baptist Church, Norfolk. It involved setting written goals in six areas:

1. Worship
2. Missions and Evangelism
3. Sunday School
4. Leadership
5. Prayer
6. Finances

We named the strategy "It's a Brand New Day." Because there were many wonderful goals, priority was given to three goals in each of these six areas, for a total of 18 goals. One year after "It's a Brand New Day" began, we had reached or were in the process of reaching 16 of the 18 goals and had our sights set on the remaining two. A church may be active, but our church is active with purpose, unity, synergy, and joy!

Step # 6: *Retool ministry and repot people.*

Most any program may be retooled with purpose. For example, if Sunday School is perceived only as a program, it will limp along with little impact. However, when Sunday School is understood as strategic, life is breathed into the organization, and revival will sweep through every class.

For Sunday School to be the force it was designed to be, retooling is often required. Getting back to the basics — enrolling prospects, starting new units and departments, providing space and training, keeping classes to manageable sizes — is essential to the strategy called Sunday School. In determining baselines, we discovered that two thousand members of our church were not enrolled in a Bible Study class! *Purpose* always calls a church back to the *basics.*

Repotting people is another important result of a ministry plan. Sometimes repotting means people switch their ministry involvement or change from one department to another. Helping people determine how they are going to be involved in ministry is vital to the success of moving a congregation from being program-based to purpose-driven ministry. The primary tool we use is called *The BodyLife Journey: Guiding Believers into Ministry*[8] (available from LifeWay Christian Resources or LifeWay Christian Stores: 0-6330-2888-6, Leader Notebook and 0-6330-2889-4, Member Notebook). This tool provides an assimilation process to help people discover their spiritual gifts, their personality, and their passion. Members connect to the vision of our church by discovering how God "wired" them, how He made them, and what they enjoy doing. We are now staffing our professional ministry team based on this plan.

Please note that this entire process took two years to accomplish. It takes six months to grow squash but sixty years to grow an oak tree. Which does your church focus on planting? There is one final step worth remembering,

Step # 7: *Evaluate systematically and comprehensively.*

A church that follows these steps is now in position to gain appropriate feedback and to see measurable results from well-planned ministry. Pastor, you may kill a program by not devoting the time, personnel, calendar space, or finances required for its success. But when a program dies, relationships are damaged, people are misunderstood, and the church suffers unnecessarily. When a program is evaluated in light of the ministry plan, people are reclaimed, ministry is revived, and the church keeps on target for God's glory in the task of making disciples in His saving name. During the process of our evaluation, our members coined a phrase that makes me smile from the inside out. It is,

Sacred cows make great hamburgers.

---

1 Robert E. Coleman, *The Master Plan of Evangelism* (Old Tappan, NJ: Fleming H. Revell, 1964), 33-34.

2 John Maxwell, *Developing the Leader Within You* (Nashville: Thomas Nelson, 1993), 26

3 James F. Engle and Wilbert Norton, *What's Gone Wrong with the Harvest?* (Grand Rapids: Zondervan, 1975), 21.

4 A. A. Milne, *Pooh Goes Visiting and Pooh and Piglet Nearly Catch a Woozle* (New York: Methuen Children's Books Ltd., 1990).

5 Milne, *Pooh Goes Visiting and Pooh and Piglet Nearly Catch a Woozle.*

6 PETA Organization: People for the Ethical Treatment of Animals

7 Glenn Bland, *Success: The Glenn Bland Method* (Wheaton: Tyndale House, 1979), 44.

8 John S. Powers, *The BodyLife Journey: Guiding Believers into Ministry* (Nashville: LifeWay, 2001)

CHAPTER 8

Mythological Mountain #6:
"The Eighty-Twenty Rule
Is the Norm."

*A*nd *He gave some as apostles, and some as prophets, and some as evangelists, and some as pastors and teachers, for the equipping of the saints for the work of service, to the building up of the body of Christ; until we all attain to the unity of the faith, and of the knowledge of the Son of God, to a mature man, to the measure of the stature which belongs to the fullness of Christ* (Ephesians 4:11-13).

As the human body has the metabolism for life and growth, it also has the limbs and organs necessary for the body to be able to function. The same is true of the church. God has given each person spiritual gifts and talents and abilities that are needed by the church. For the church to function with maximum effectiveness, it is essential that each person use his gifts, talents, and abilities for the good of the body. By God's design, not even the smallest or most insignificant part of the body is unessential. This is true of both the universal and local church. Each person in the body of Christ has been put there by God and has been given spiritual gifts, talents, and abilities that are essential to the life of the total body. It is impossible for a person to live normally without one arm or one eye or three fingers, as it is for the body of Christ to function unless each of its parts is functioning properly.[1]

Climbing to the pinnacle of the wind-swept summit known as Everest is rarely done alone. Reinhold Messner was the first man to complete a solo ascent in 1980, climbing via the North East Ridge to the North Face of Chomolungma. Two years earlier Messner entered the record books when he climbed to the top of the world without the aid of oxygen. Even the most experienced and dedicated high-altitude climbers do not attempt such a dangerous feat.

Most contemporary mountaineers who express interest in climbing Everest pay $65,000 each, which covers the cost of items necessary to bag the summit. In addition to a professional guide, Sherpas — highly trained natives who have been employed for the rigors of extreme altitude climbing — are also connected to the party. A Sherpa's responsibility is to carry equipment, food, water, and oxygen from one site to another. These strong men have been known to carry additional items such as televisions, radios, cell phones, and even computers. Sherpas go ahead of the expedition party and mark the trail, securing the aluminum ladders across the deep fissures in glacier ice known as "crevasses." They also set up five campsites, along the grand valley of ice known as the Western Cwm (pronounced *koom*). Cwm is a Welsh term for "valley or crique" and was named by George Mallory, who first saw it during the initial Everest expedition in 1921. Expedition parties from around the globe vie for position on the mountain. During certain times of the year, there are dozens of people crawling all over Everest.

The point is, whether they are inexperienced amateurs or world-class veterans of this peak, for obvious reasons a mountaineer is rarely left alone on the face of Everest. The odds of surviving a push to the snow-capped summit of Everest improve greatly when a trekker surrounds him or herself with a team of people committed to the same goal.

Local churches could learn from the expertise of these daring dreamers. While we are talking about learning, consider the habits of geese.

Lessons from the Geese[2]

As each bird flaps its wings, it creates an "uplift" for the bird following. By flying in a V formation, the whole flock adds 71% more flying range than if each bird flew alone.

LESSON: *People who share a common direction and sense of community can get where they are going quicker and easier because they are traveling on the thrust of one another.*

Whenever a goose falls out of formation, it suddenly feels the drag and resistance of trying to fly alone, and quickly gets back into formation to take advantage of the "lifting power" of the bird immediately in front.

LESSON: *It pays to take turns doing hard tasks and sharing leadership responsibilities in an interdependent relationship.*

Geese in formation honk from behind to encourage those up front to keep up their speed.

LESSON: *We need to be sure our honking from behind is encouraging, not something less helpful.*

When a goose gets sick, wounded, or shot down, two geese drop out of formation and follow him down to help and protect him. They stay with him until he is either able to fly again or dies. Then they launch out on their own, to join with another formation or to catch up with their flock.

LESSON: *If we have as much sense as the geese, we'll stand by each other like that.*

Both geese and thin-air mountaineers have a grasp on a vital principle that some local churches tend to avoid. Ask any member who has been connected to the body of Christ, and he can pretty well define the components of the next mythological mountain. This summary is simply called "the eighty-twenty rule."

When it comes to the local church, what is "the eighty-twenty rule?" If you had to write your definition, what would it be?

Was your answer similar to either of the statements below? "The eighty-twenty rule" goes something like this:

- Eighty percent of the work in a local church is accomplished by twenty percent of the people.
- Eighty percent of the money given through a local church is given by twenty percent of the people.

Some answer incorrectly because they have not been in a local church long enough to be taught "the eighty-twenty rule" by those who accept it and live by it. Others may miss giving the correct response because they didn't know such a "rule" exists. They didn't know where to look for the answer.

You are thinking to yourself, "Obviously, this rule is written somewhere in stone isn't it?" No! "Then it translates from the ancient biblical texts, right?" Wrong again! You say, "I know, I know, the Bible has lots of rules, like the Golden Rule and this is one of them, correct?" Sorry, this "rule" is not found in the Bible. "It is possible that the fathers of our faith passed it down through verbal tradition, true?" Absolutely untrue!

You are wondering, "So, if it is not written down somewhere for us to research and if the Bible is silent about this rule and if the fathers of the faith didn't pass it on, where did "the eighty-twenty rule" begin?" Remember our definition of a myth?

A notion based more on tradition or convenience than upon fact.

The so-called "eighty-twenty rule" is pure myth. Is it true in some churches? Yes, but it relies on tradition that has no biblical basis. It is perpetuated by members who seek ways to remain carnally convenient rather than ways to build their Christian character. This myth has become a stronghold for mediocrity within too many members of the local church. Whenever the spiritual heat is turned up, these members rush to a fall-back position, "Pastor, now you *know* that eighty percent of the money given and work done around here is through twenty per-cent of the people." While this may be true of a given congregation, it is still unacceptable. We should neither legitimize nor promote such an idea by continuing to speak of it as fact.

First, *"the eighty-twenty rule" is presumptuous.*

This mythological rule assumes too much. Left to its own, this notion will continue being the primary excuse for nominal living and ordinary thinking by members of local churches. It presumes that believers, new and mature, want to live an inferior life for Jesus. This myth chokes life from potential ministry like a wolf strangles a lamb. It presumes that Spirit-filled Christians do not want to swim against the wicked currents of this world. It fails to boldly declare, "If you walk with the world, you can't walk with God." It intimates that what a believer has to offer is unimportant to the kingdom and disinteresting to a watching world. In contrast, the evangelist D. L. Moody once said,

"This one thing I do," said Paul. If he had folded his arms and said,

"O dear, the Christians are so cold we cannot do anything; if the Church was wide awake we might." Never you mind whether the church is wide-awake or not; you keep wide-awake yourself. If you wait for the church you will never do anything. I made up my mind ten years ago that I would go on as if there were not another man in the world but me to do the work. I knew I had to give my account of stewardship. I suppose they say of me, "he is a radical; he is a fanatic; he only has one idea." Well, it is a glorious idea. I would rather have that said of me than be a man of ten thousand ideas and do nothing with them. To have one idea, and that idea is Christ, that is the man for me; that is the man we want now. A man that has one idea, one desire, one thought, and that idea, that thought, that desire Christ and Him crucified — that is what this groaning, perishing world wants now. It can get on without rhetoric; it can get on without our fine speeches, without our eloquence. It does not want them; it wants Christ and Him crucified.[3]

Second, *"the eighty-twenty rule" is predictable.*

When a church chooses to operate under the weight of this myth, zeal for ministry will be tempered. How smart is the businessman who employs one hundred workers, yet allows the overwhelming majority of the work to be done by a minority of his employees? We would say, "not smart." The same holds true in the local church. It is reasonable to expect members, *all* members, to join in the work of ministry. A church gets what it expects. Expectations and involvement rise and fall together. If a church expects involvement from people, it gets involvement from people! If expectations for members are nonexistent, the results are predictable, almost to the person.

Third, *"the eighty-twenty rule" is problematic.*

A church that adopts this myth as "gospel" unnecessarily creates a whole series of problems for the congregation. The devil understands the impact of a church that is unified. He saw it at Pentecost and Antioch.

104

That's why the cunning sleight (deception) of the devil is to divide us that he may destroy us. What problems are inherent with accepting "the eighty-twenty rule?" For starters, members become casual about the things of God. The work of ministry cannot expand because of limited resources. Giving is hindered. I have wondered if the debt local churches carry could be laid at the feet of this mythological bandit. If God's people just *tithed*, many churches that struggle financially would experience a freedom to expand their ministry.

Let's see how the "rule" impacts a church that receives one million dollars toward its budget. Hypothetically, if eighty-percent of the offerings are given by twenty-percent of God's people, $800,000 dollars is given by those twenty percent. However, when 100% of the members are expected to *tithe*, the total amount of money given to the budget would be four million dollars. Financially, the devil is dividing us. Consider also the impact on workers in ministry. "A few good men" may be the motto for the Marines, but God's army calls for every saint "to do the work of ministry."

Fourth, *"the eighty-twenty rule" is unbiblical, but also prophetic.*

This notion flies in the face of the gospel. It scoffs at the bloody sacrifice of Jesus. Expecting only twenty-percent of God's people to be active in a local church grieves the Spirit of God. Such mediocrity quenches His activity. It also makes a believer's heart vulnerable for attack by the adversary. "A Christian in his ignorance may be deceived by the powers of darkness, may unwittingly tumble into the trap of Satan, and fulfill the conditions for his working."[4]

Upon reflection, there is *one* place the Bible uses percentages of this nature. All three of the synoptic Gospels record the parable of the soils. (Matthew 13:1-9; 18-23; Mark 4:1-20; Luke 8:4-15). Jesus spoke in parables, that is, He laid truth alongside everyday life, so that His listeners might understand Him. Laying this parable alongside the contemporary church has a sobering effect. Good soil and an abiding believer have similar characteristics. Both produce fruit! However, in the same field are three other soils. One is "hard," one is "rocky," and the third is "thorny." Could it be that this myth is like a counter-agent? Could it be that those who adhere to it reveal what kind of faith they possess? If that is the case, it seems logical that only those members who bear fruit are truly believers. That's one out of four, or twenty-five percent. The remaining are living under the deception that they are Christians; however, their profession and practice do not square; their lips and their lives are in perpetual spiritual disconnect.

If this analysis is valid, the local church must address this myth before it is *eternally* too late for those who are falling prey to it. Once the great evangelist Billy Graham was asked, "Dr. Graham, do you believe half of the members of a church are lost?" Graham replied, "No, I believe about eighty percent of them are."

Maybe that is why the percentages remain so skewed. Oh God, Your church, Your people need reviving!

SETTING OUR SIGHTS FOR THE SUMMIT

A thin-air mountaineer can expect to visit five different camps on his way to conquering the treacherous, icy peak of Everest. But in all probability he will not do it alone. He will require a guide. That is true for bagging this mythological mountain, too. We need a guide to follow, a model by which to measure ourselves, something or someone to copy.

There is such a spiritual escort. All the basic ingredients that the Savior desires in a church were found in the Thessalonian congregation. The letter the Apostle Paul wrote to these saints lays out a pattern for the contemporary church to replicate.

Constantly bearing in mind your work of faith and labor of love and steadfastness of hope in our Lord Jesus Christ in the presence of our God and Father, knowing, brethren beloved by God, His choice of you; for our gospel did not come to you in word only, but also in power and in the Holy Spirit and with full conviction; just as you know what kind of men we proved to be among you for your sake. You also became imitators of us and of the Lord, having received the word in much tribulation with the joy of the Holy Spirit, so that you became an example to all the believers in Macedonia and in Achaia. For the word of the Lord has sounded forth from you, not only in Macedonia and Achaia, but also in every place your faith toward God has gone forth, so that we have no need to say anything (1 Thessalonians 1:3-8).

A church that believes and accepts the notion called "the eighty-twenty rule" is an unhealthy church in many aspects. We may learn something about ourselves by comparing these first century saints to the contemporary church. A careful study of the Thessalonian church reveals all the qualities found in a healthy congregation. We will benefit from some important background information. The preacher from Tarsus first proclaimed the gospel to these Thessalonians during his second missionary journey. After leaving them, he sent Timothy to see how they were faring. Timothy returned with a fantastic report. That news prompted this first epistle from Paul. Notice what he didn't share:

- No reference is given to membership numbers.
- There is no mention of a ministry plan with goals and objectives.
- Nothing is said about church programming.
- Paul does not commend their worship style or any special projects.
- Other than Timothy, no character references are given for any person.

However, Paul provides important principles or keys to help us see the kind of church the Lord Jesus expects in the twenty-first century. Such truth will assist us in bagging this horrible and mythological mindset called "the eighty-twenty rule."

First, *we are to be devoted to Jesus* (1 Thessalonians 2:13).

One does not have to read very far to see that these members were rightly connected to the Lord Jesus. They were "in God the Father and the Lord Jesus Christ" (1 Thessalonians 1:1) and gave evidence of an intimate relationship. Herein lies the first secret to overcoming this icy, mythological mountain. Our problem is that we are trying to get unredeemed people into the work of ministry reserved only for the redeemed. Ineffectiveness in the local church may be traced back to enlisting members who are unsaved, unsure, and therefore unqualified to do the work of ministry. Like these early saints, we are to be devoted to Jesus.

According to Acts 17, Paul spent only three Sabbaths in Thessalonica (v. 2). But from the very beginning the response to the preaching of the gospel was incredible. Verse 4 highlights that response,

> *And some of them were persuaded and joined Paul and Silas, along with a great multitude of the God-fearing Greeks and a number of the leading women.*

These saints were devoted to Christ and to the Word of God. It seems the contemporary church is afraid to "speak the truth in love" for fear that new believers, the formerly unchurched, may not be able to handle such preaching or even desire it. In some of his most recent research, Thom Rainer challenges such notions. He found:

- The formerly unchurched *do* desire doctrinal depth. Ninety-eight percent of those interviewed want to delve deeper into Scripture from their first day in the church.

- The formerly unchurched *don't* care about the name of the church. Eighty-eight percent of those studied never considered the name when coming to the church. Eight percent said the name was a positive factor. Only 4 percent were negatively affected by the name.

- The formerly unchurched *are* attracted to Sunday School. They are 20 percent more active in Sunday School than previously-churched Christians.

- The formerly unchurched *are* attracted to convictional preaching.[5]

It was true of the believers in Thessalonica; it's still true today. "Those whom God chooses, He changes."[6] One of the differences is the believers' attitude toward the Scriptures. Just as at Pentecost, God's Word had life-changing impact on the saints at Thessalonica.

We need to get into God's Word and allow God's Word to get into us. Doing so will lead us to reject mediocre living that has been birthed out of mythological thinking.

Second, *we are to duplicate Christlikeness* (1 Thessalonians 1:6a).

These saints "became imitators of us and of the Lord." The Greek term translated "imitators" is *mimetes,* from which the English word *mimic* is derived. They mimicked the lives of Paul, Silas, and Timothy. They imitated Jesus. A second key to overcoming this myth is unity. Unity in the body of Christ would be unquestionable if everyone were in pursuit of being like Jesus. A. W. Tozer taught that if a hundred pianos were tuned to each other, their pitch would not be very accurate. But if they were all tuned to one tuning fork, they would automatically be tuned to each other.[7] The believer's desire should be to adjust his life to that of the Lord Jesus and not to those around him, especially uncommitted men and women.

Third, *we are to pay a price … joyfully* (1 Thessalonians 1:6b).

These Thessalonians were not having a garden party with their faith. It was not *convenient* for them to live for Jesus. Many of them had to break away from pagan religions. These new converts had to leave the Jewish synagogue. Everyone paid a price to be a part of this local church.

A third key to overcoming this myth is sacrifice. Acts 17:5-6 gives thrilling insight into the power of sacrifice. The instant Paul and Silas opened their mouths about the risen Christ, Satan reared his ugly head in the form of trouble, persecution, and societal pressure. It wasn't just mild opposition they faced, but tremendous strain. The testimony of the pagans is particularly interesting. They were shouting,

"These men who have upset the world have come here also."

The fervency of Paul and Silas' faith turned their world upside down. The world could not avoid them, stop them, nor even slow them down. Any local church that is committed to exposing sin will do the same. Preaching the risen Lord Jesus always irritates wickedness, so we should come to expect it, "with the joy of the Holy Spirit" (1 Thessalonians 1:6b).

Fourth, *we are to exhibit an encouraging testimony* (1 Thessalonians 1:7-8).

Paul commended these first century saints by saying, "You became an example to all the believers in Macedonia and in Achaia." Their testimony was so pure that it encouraged other believers. Christians either encourage or discourage one another. Paul used the believers in Macedonia to encourage the rich Corinthians to participate in the Jerusalem offering. Sometime earlier the same Macedonians had received encouragement from the saints in Thessalonica. This encouragement was singular and churchwide. Everyone was involved. Everyone gladly contributed to maintaining a stellar witness for Christ.

Their collective testimony of God's word had "sounded forth." The Greek word is *exechetai*, from which we get the English word *echo*. Here is a fourth key to bagging this myth. We do not make up the message; we must echo His truth. Doing so encourages people to live for Jesus. The writer of Hebrews teaches us to "consider how to stimulate one another to love and good deeds" (10:24). A commitment to stimulating and encouraging members is another way to ascend to the top of this summit.

Fifth, *we are to live expectantly for Christ's return* (1 Thessalonians 1:10).

A summit assault on Mount Everest is filled with expectancy. The same kind of anticipation should reside in the hearts of members of churches. Our faces should be set, our minds made up, and our gaits quickening. Our eyes should be fixed on one thing, the coming of the Lord Jesus Christ. Every church that is truly committed to being what God wants it to be must be aware that Jesus is coming. Allowing this myth to live in the hearts of churches means many members will not be waiting for Him. When I think about His return, the urgency to be even more effective for Jesus rushes over me. Time is growing shorter by the day. Every member is needed in the task of delivering the ungodly from "the wrath to come." It's time to take stock of the membership of our churches. I fear many church members may hear the horrific words of the Judge who will say,

I never knew you; depart from Me, you who practice lawlessness (Matthew 7:23).

If we are going to set our sights for this summit, we must be willing to become the church where every member joins together to bring honor to the Lord Jesus. That's the way it worked in Paul's day. I believe it can happen again. Ron and Patricia Owens wrote a song that expresses our need well.

> *Lord, do it again, Lord, do it again,*
> *Pour out Your Spirit upon us, Lord, do it again,*
> *Lord, do it again, Lord, do it again,*
> *Send us a mighty revival, Lord, do it again!* [8]

[1] W. A. Criswell, *The Doctrine of the Church* (Nashville: Convention Press, 1980), 44-45.

[2] Popular Anecdote, Source Unknown.

[3] Stanley and Patricia Gundry, *The Wit and Wisdom of D. L. Moody* (Chicago: Moody Press, 1974), 62-63.

[4] Watchman Nee, *The Spiritual Man: Volume I* (New York: Christian Fellowship Publishers, 1968), 97.

[5] Thom Rainer, *New Insights to Reaching the Unchurched* (Fuller Theological Seminary: Tape # 7031, Vol. 92).

[6] Warren W. Wiersbe, *Be Ready* (Wheaton: Victor Books, 1979), 26.

[7] John F. MacArthur, Jr., *Shepherdology* (John F. MacArthur, Jr., 1989), 81.

[8] Ron and Patricia Owens, "Lord, Do It Again!" Copyright 1981 by Ron Owens. Used by permission.

CHAPTER 9

Mythological Mountain #7:
"Belonging to a local
Church Is Not Important."

N*o one will push hard against your breastbone and say, "Shape up your life. Get with it. You say you're a Christian? Walk like it. You've done wrong? Confess it and come back to God." No one else does that. Only the church. I'll add more — only those who continue faithfully in attendance of church services will hear reproof and exhortation and encouragement and rebuke that will help keep their lives in line. In fact, I recently came up with a list of four special benefits of church attendance:*

- *Accountability*
- *Consistency*
- *Unity*
- *Stability*

What I have observed is that Christians who lose faith in the local church and walk away, saying, "No thanks, I don't need it," have struggles, without exception, in one or more of these areas — sometimes all four. They lose (or wish to lose) accountability. They lack consistency in their walk. They cultivate an independent spirit, rather than an interdependence of love and concern. And when pressure strikes, they lack stability. Why? The answer isn't that complicated: There's no family around.[1]

A bookkeeper from New Zealand named Edmund Hillary, with his climbing companion Tenzing Norgay, made history by reaching the top of Mount Everest on May 29, 1953. Returning to tell the tale, they thought the world's highest peak would no longer entice climbers. "We thought that since we'd climbed it, people would lose interest," says Hillary, now eighty-one years of age. This has proven to be an uncharacteristic misjudgment. According to the American Alpine Club, the summit has been visited more than 1,000 times since.

The most common trail to the top of the world involves conquering several distinguishable milestones. After leaving the base camp, hikers are introduced to the Khumbu Icefall, the most technically demanding section on the entire route. Because the movement of this glacier has been measured at between three and four feet per day, no part of the South Col is feared more by climbers than the Icefall. Hikers maneuver under, around, and over these tottering blocks of ice called *seracs*, some as large as office buildings. Climbing through these unstable towers of ice is much like playing Russian roulette. In 1963, Jake Breitenbach was the Icefall's first victim. Since then, eighteen other climbers have died as a result of a falling serac.

Next is The Western Cwm, also called the "Valley of Silence." Here, climbers get their first glimpse of Everest's upper slopes. Some of the most difficult days on Everest are in the Western Cwm, when on a windless day it is desperately hot. David Breshears says, "You literally pray for a puff of wind or a cloud to cover the sun so you can keep moving up to Advance Base Camp."

The Lhoste Face is also an unavoidable part of the traditional southeast route up Everest. Camp Three sits about halfway up this ascending wall of glacial blue ice. The entire route is fixed with ropes, and climbers must get into the rhythmic movement of pulling and stepping up. Kicking steps while lodging one's front points into the hard blue ice is the predominant movement required for this unrelenting ascent.

The first rock a climber touches on the way up Everest is the sedimentary sandstone of the Yellow Band. Then comes the Geneva Spur, named by the Swiss in 1952, which is the last major hurdle before reaching the last camp on Everest. The South Col is the site of Camp Four and is used by all expeditions as the high camp. A demanding 3,000 feet still remain from here to the summit. At this elevation, all expedition and Sherpa members sleep with a low flow of oxygen, except those who dream of attempting the summit "gas free." Sitting at 27,700 feet is the next hurdle called "The Balcony," a platform for climbers to rest on and admire the scenic view of the sun as it rises in the east. One thousand feet higher is the South Summit — the hikers' point of no return.

Then comes the terrifying Cornice Traverse, a knife-edge of snow plastered to intermittent rocks. Fixed ropes are the only protection in this most exposed section of the climb. A misstep to the right sends a climber tumbling down the 10,000 foot Kangshung Face. A misstep to the left sends one careening 8,000 feet down the Southwest Face. The most famous physical feature on Everest, the Hillary Step, at 28,750 feet, is a forty-foot spur of snow and ice. It is the last obstacle barring access to the gently angled summit slopes. The summit is at 29,035 feet and is the world's highest point. It is covered with prayer flags, remnants of survey equipment, and personal mementos. The summit is about the size of a picnic table. On a clear day, it seems as if one can see across half a continent from this vantage point.

A local church that decides to climb a mythological mountain meets with arduous work. The base of another mountain-sized notion greets us with its cocky, cavalier attitude that says, "Belonging to a local church is not important." Why blaze a trail to attempt the summit of this mountain? As Mallory said, "Because it is there!" What are the characteristics of a membership that adopts a notion like this?

To help us understand the mindset "belonging to a local church is unimportant," consider with me some oxymorons like: cold sweat, jumbo shrimp, bad luck, clean dirt, dry ice, deafening silence, holy wars, kosher ham, .999 pure, rolling stop, safe sex, tax return, vaguely aware, and zero deficit.

One oxymoron used in the ranks of the local church is: *non-resident member*. What does this mean? Who are these people? How does the term (and the people it represents) impact the local church? Non-resident members are members of a local church who have moved such a distance from the church that their involvement is impacted negatively. This move may be the result of job change, illness, retirement, etc. For whatever reason, these members move away and do not reconnect to another congregation. They represent the notion that being a member of a local church is unimportant. Though records vary from church to church, non-resident status often represents as much as one-half of the total membership of older congregations.

Imagine the President of the United States calling upon the armed forces only to discover five out of ten soldiers could not be located. The public might call this status "unprepared." The military calls this status "absent without leave" (AWOL). Imagine one-half of the employees of a Fortune 500 company not showing up for work on any given day. The marketplace calls this behavior "unemployed." What would you call it? What would we think of parents with two sons, but because of their carelessness, one of the boys is misplaced or lost? Social workers might call these parents "unfit."

Imagine what the God of glory thinks of a local church that no longer knows where half of its members are? We do not know their spiritual need or condition; we are oblivious to their hurts. Like a shepherd who loses half his flock, how hollow is it saying to Him, "Lord, we lost them"? Beloved, this mythological mountain must be conquered and quickly. Within the membership of most local churches reside four "types" of Christians.

First, *carnal Christians*

After some members connect to a local church, they continue living in the flesh, unchallenged by their status as members. It is difficult distinguishing them from unsaved people. In fact, some theologians believe in all probability, these members are unsaved. However, Paul described these members as *brethren*. One thing cannot be denied. The attitudes and actions of these members surely resemble those who have not experienced spiritual transformation. Look at additional characteristics of carnal believers in 1 Corinthians 3:1-3.

> *And I, brethren, could not speak to you as to spiritual men, but as to men of flesh, as to babes in Christ. I gave you milk to drink, not solid food; for you were not yet able to receive it. Indeed, even now you are not yet able, for you are still fleshly. For since there is jealousy and strife among you, are you not fleshly, and are you not walking like mere men?*

What a description! These members had succumbed to the enticing pressures of their own flesh. Even after several years of being in the local church, these believers were not growing. They were babies in the faith as illustrated by their spiritual diet. They were drinking milk, when they should have been eating solid foods. Their spiritual digestive systems remained weak. They were unable to handle even the most elementary truths of doctrine. Nothing is more precious than a baby; nothing is more heart-breaking than a thirty-year-old with the mind of a child. Notice Paul said they were *still* fleshly. Their spiritual condition was inexcusable. They had been believers long enough to have grown up, but they continued *walking like mere men.*

One reason the local church seems to struggle in the trenches of mediocrity is due in part to members who refuse to grow in their walk with Jesus. They may attend every Sunday but remain inactive and ineffective for the Lord. They sit in church with closed minds, closed Bibles, and closed hearts.

Second, *culturally stunted Christians*

Culturally stunted Christians are those members who sacrifice future ministry because they continue living in the past. They reflect on and live in "the good ol' days." Mark Twain once said, "The trouble with our times is that the future is not what it used to be." Sometimes they are guilty of forsaking solid biblical foundations. Terms like "relevance" are used to describe ministry, worship, teaching, and even preaching. It is at this point we need the reminder that God's Word remains relevant. Some members who bow to their culture falsely think that a strong church is the result of technique. Neither our wisdom, power-point presentations, sermon-note forms, music, nor any other style of communication makes the Bible relevant. A Bible-believing church is born when the Spirit of God moves in the hearts of His people. A church is weakened by the notion of members who revel in the past or who attempt to bring contemporary culture and church together in an unhealthy and even unholy manner. Such members seek to make their church convenient for them. Like Old Testament Israel, these saints tend to drift away from devotion to the Lord and relegate the ministries of the church to a marketing tool. See if you recognize these identifying marks.

- *Their faith* is a religion based on popular interpretation of Scripture. This faith is based on good works and intentions.
- *Their view of Scripture* is that it is a collection of guidelines, allegories, myths, and stories useful for good living. Offensive verses are often ignored.
- *Their goal* is to seek approval of people. Don't offend the world; don't offend the community; don't offend people.
- *Their view of sin* is that it is a normal part of life. Ignore sin, or you may offend someone. They deal with sin by trying to do better next time; never make anyone feel guilty.
- *Their care for people* is by rejecting uncompromising Christians who might offend someone. Do to others as you would have others do to you.
- *Their outreach methods* are to get along with people — adapt the church to the community so that everyone will feel at home.

Such a mentality produces mediocre faith that fosters indifference and apathy about the things of God as well as the true mission and ministry of the local church.

Third, *casual Christians*

You may have heard about the guy who complained to his wife about the music at their church. "Honey," he said, "I am so tired of the same old music. Every time I go to church, we either sing "Away in a Manger" or "Up from the Grave He Arose.""

Casual Christians are those folks who use the local church when it is beneficial to them. They come to church when it is *expected*. Weddings, funerals, Easter, and Christmas are times when casual Christians appear. Their contributions are criticism. Their walk with God becomes flippant and relaxed. Like hibernating bears, they are comfortable and do not want to be disturbed. Like calloused skin, their hearts have layers of hardness after years of living tepidly for the Lord. The Laodicean church typifies these church members. Not hot nor cold, they are lukewarm. It's not that they don't believe the doctrines of the faith; they are not opposed to evangelizing the world. These members aren't opponents of the Lord; they are just indifferent to Him and to those things He deems vitally important.

Fourth, *committed Christians*

If a mountaineer is to successfully climb Everest, he cannot be flippant about the journey. He couldn't care less how the culture perceives his task, and if he is to survive the struggles to the summit, he will certainly be focused with an intensity rarely experienced in his life. If the local church is to overcome the mythological mountain that church membership is not important, similar passion is required of its members. It will not be casual, culturally stunted, or carnal Christians who will bag this mountain. Only one kind of saint makes it into thin-air living for Jesus. That saint is a committed Christian.

SETTING OUR SIGHTS FOR THE SUMMIT

Some people correctly call this condition "normal Christianity." Pentecost equipped the apostles with power from heaven. When Peter finished preaching his first sermon, the Spirit's ministry of convicting of sin, righteousness, and judgment to come was evident, and thousands of people were saved. The historian Luke records,

> So then, those who had received his word were baptized; and there were added that day about three thousand souls. And they were continually devoting themselves to the apostles' teaching and to fellowship, to the breaking of bread and to prayer. And everyone kept feeling a sense of awe; and many wonders and signs were taking place through the

apostles. And all those who had believed were together, and had all things in common; and they began selling their property and possessions, and were sharing them with all, as anyone might have need. And day by day continuing with one mind in the temple, and breaking bread from house to house, they were taking their meals together with gladness and sincerity of heart, praising God, and having favor with all the people. And the Lord was adding to their number day by day those who were being saved (Acts 2:41-47).

These first century spiritual hikers are a great pattern for the contemporary church member to model. If we would capture their enthusiasm for involvement in the local church, this myth — belonging to a local church is not important — would become as antiquated as a 45 RPM record. What made these members so special? Four factors contributed to their enthusiasm.

First, *a spirit of repentance was evident* (Acts 2:38-40).

Peter told them how to be saved. These listeners repented of their sin and placed their trust in Jesus Christ. Furthermore, they gave proof of the sincerity of their faith and repentance by following the Lord in believer's baptism. They were baptized "in the name of Jesus Christ." Their membership was strong from the beginning because no member was ashamed of identifying publicly with the Savior.

When it comes to meaningful membership, the local church that expects a sinner to make a public profession of faith is building a quality of sincerity in the heart of the new believer. Today, there is a shifting from this biblical practice to accommodate people and increase membership numbers. Some churches allow people to join over the phone; it won't be long before they are faxing their membership into the church office. Other churches reject a public invitation for an inquiry room or home visit.

What is lost when a church receives members in such a fashion? One thing is a visual of spiritual brokenness. Tear-off commitment cards are never a replacement for salty tears. Other men and women with whom the Holy Spirit is dealing need to see and hear the process of becoming a Christian. Following the Lord in believer's baptism is also part of the process. The Spirit of God uses sinners who receive the free gift of eternal life to convict other sinners who need similar grace.

To design the activities of the church to appeal to unbelievers, or to allow them to play a major role in the life of the church, is to give them a false sense of security. The result for them may be eternal tragedy. The church must reach out in love to those who do not know Christ. It must never, however, let them feel that they are a part of the fellowship until they come to faith in Christ. And no evangelistic purpose should ever be undertaken that alters what the church is by divine design — an assembly of saved worshipers pursuing holiness and spiritual service.2

Second, *a spirit of discipleship was apparent* (Acts 2:41-42).

Three thousand people were saved and baptized on the day the church was born. But rather than having those children on a park bench and leaving them there, the early church was committed to discipling. They did more than make converts; they discipled these new believers. These members were fully devoted to Jesus.

- *They were excited to hear the Word.* These saints prioritized hearing God's Word proclaimed and explained. God's Word is foundational to the growth and health of every church. Members cannot operate on truth that remains untaught. That's why there must be resolve in pastors to expound God's Word with clarity and application to contemporary believers.

- *They were committed to unity.* A congregation with half of its membership absent is not exactly the picture of unity that our Lord desires. For a Christian to fail to participate in the local church is reprehensible. In fact, members who choose to isolate themselves are living in disobedience. Hebrews 10:24-25 clearly teaches that we are to exhort one another to "love and good deeds, not forsaking our own assembling together." From the Greek term *koinonia*, fellowship means "partnering, sharing, cooperating, participating, and contributing." Someone defined fellowship as "two fellows in the same ship." Members of the early church were in the same boat and were committed to it.

- *They were confronting sin within.* That's the purpose of the Lord's Supper according to 1 Corinthians 11. The Supper calls for self-examination and purging of one's sin. As each member participates in the breaking of bread, the church remains purified. Nothing sweeps sin out of the church like true reflection on the cross of Jesus.

- *They were involved in concerted prayer.* Many members today are practical atheists. They believe in God but act as if He does not exist. This blind spot shows up clearly when it comes to the discipline of prayer. Call a fast and no one comes; call a feed and everyone comes. Some members will show up for concerts, comics, and even to hear how famous converts received Christ, but prayer meeting remains low priority for them. Could a member's devotion to the local church be linked to the church's devotion to concerted prayer? The church was born in a prayer meeting. In fact, the apostles prayed ten days, preached ten minutes, and three thousand people were saved. Today, we preach ten days, pray ten minutes, and wonder why the Lord doesn't bless!

These committed Christians were devoted to ongoing repentance and discipleship.

Third, *a spirit of expectation was normal* (Acts 2:43-47a).

The early church recognized when God was in the house. They had *phobos*, reverential fear of divine presence. Whether inside the fellowship or outside in the pagan pool, people stood up to take notice, not of their programs or their slick presentations but of their reverence of Holy God. Members of the early church knew how to worship, and worship they did! As a result of their fear, God performed miracles. In fact, their fear and God's moving were connected. The more they feared the Lord, the more God moved. Today, the greatest miracle is when God moves a sinner to come to Christ in repentance and salvation.

The early church did not need a capital fund campaign because everyone was involved in giving to the work of ministry. No need went unmet. There was gladness not sadness in the church because there were no hidden agendas. Agendas are to churches what a reef is to a ship. Left undetected, the church will likely be damaged.

Fourth, *a spirit of multiplication was continual* (Acts 2:47b).

Their commitment to unity (2:44) and their dedication to ministry that magnified the Lord (2:47a) had results. "The Lord was adding to their number day by day those who were being saved" (2:47b). The watching world was blown away by the lifestyle of these fully devoted followers of Jesus. They saw how members treated one another. They marveled at their fellowship and hearty service for the Lord. It so impressed them that many of them came to the Savior as a result of these members who simply walked with Jesus in continual revival.

The myth that declares "belonging to a local church is unimportant" just wasn't the case for these New Testament believers. It was important to them. This imperative applies to contemporary believers. Jesus wrote a letter to a group of saints. In it He commended their zeal for ministry, their sacrifice in service, and their theological purity. But He had one thing against them, "that you have left your first love" (Revelation 2:4). About thirty years earlier, the Apostle Paul commended this same congregation for its loving nature when he wrote,

> For this reason I too, having heard of the faith in the Lord Jesus which exists among you, and your love for all the saints, do not cease giving thanks for you, while making mention of you in my prayers (Ephesians 1:15-16).

But for some reason, these believers had left their first love. It was not an accident. It was intentional and continual, and the Lord Jesus exposed their loveless actions. In the same way, the contemporary church needs a visit from heaven and a fresh touch of His power.

This mythological mountain can be overtaken. We can win the battle for the summit of this mistaken notion. But it will take believers with a wholesale commitment to the Lord Jesus and His local church. The church is an assembly. When thinking of assembly, my mind replays the tape of all the Christmas Eves I have spent assembling gifts and toys for my son. Maybe it's time to hang a huge sign on the front of the church that reads "Assembly Required." We are seeing what happens when it is not required!

The way we do church today makes about as much sense as "government intelligence," "an objective opinion," and "paid volunteers." In time, a local church can be better; it can be what God intended. Members will demonstrate that belonging to their church is vitally important. Such members will live in such a way that the church will evoke a positive, welcome response from this world.

---

[1] Charles R. Swindoll, *Growing Deep in the Christian Life* (Portland, OR: Multnomah Press, 1986), 361-362.

[2] John MacArthur, Jr., *The MacArthur New Testament Commentary: Acts 1-12* (Chicago: Moody Press, 1994), 82.

Conclusion

The View Is Great from the Top!

During an interview with Edmund Hillary, the famous mountain climber was asked to reflect on what he remembered most vividly about his summit assault on Everest some forty-six years earlier. He said:

There are two things I remember clearly, even in the short time I was there. One is that I did look around a bit to see if there was any sign of the remnants of Mallory [English climber George Leigh Mallory who disappeared in 1924 above the 27,700 foot level]. I didn't expect there to be, of course, after all those years. And there wasn't. The other thing is that while standing on top of Everest, I looked across the valley, toward the other great peak Makalu, and mentally worked out a route about how it could be climbed. That was the route the French first climbed it by some years later. But it showed me that even though I was standing on top of the world, it wasn't the end of everything for me, by any means. I was still looking beyond to other interesting challenges. I'll always remember doing that. I found it quite interesting.

Years ago, the Lord introduced mountains to two well-known Old Testament saints. One is a sad picture of disobedience. Moses was invited to the top of a mountain to view the Promised Land, but the great leader was unable to go into the land that flowed with milk and honey because he disobeyed God in the wilderness.

The other story is a message of victory and obedience. Caleb cried out to Joshua, "Give me this mountain!" How might we claim these mythological mountains? How do we lead our churches into the realms of thin-air living?

First, *correctly assimilate members into the church.*

This is one of the benefits of the member assimilation process called, *The BodyLife Journey: Guiding Believers into Ministry.* After years of testing and hundreds of written evaluations, *The BodyLife Journey* is proving to be a tool to help the fellowship of First Baptist Church, Norfolk, Virginia, overcome mythological mountains.

- We are overcoming the myth *"the church is a volunteer organization"* by calling every member to identify and participate in personal ministry. Our proactive position has created a positive response, and God's people are rising to the challenge. The attitude "membership equals ministry" is replacing the misguided thinking that church membership is based on personal whims and agendas.

128

- We are aggressively addressing the notion *"we must manipulate members into ministry"* by matching their spiritual gifts, personalities, and passion to unique ministry opportunity. One of our core values clearly states, "We expect every member to join us in ministering." Members are rising to this expectation.

- We deal with the perception *"we cannot place expectations on church members"* by asking, "Why not?" We refuse to allow carnal, culturally stunted, or casual members to set the direction for our fellowship. In fact, *The BodyLife Journey* is a required step of membership, immediately following a believer's profession of faith and believer's baptism. The very few who do *not* choose to become a part of our fellowship because of this expectation are still loved and welcomed. However, because we have set our sights for the summit and refuse to remain mediocre, the overwhelming majority of people have discovered how much they enjoy serving, giving, and going for Jesus.

- We speak to the concept of *"discipleship and evangelism are two separate issues"* by illustrating how evangelism grows out of a life devoted to Jesus. From the beginning of their Christian experience with us, members are challenged to develop a consistent and ongoing walk with the Lord. It's out of spiritual transformation that our members share the reason of the hope that is within them.

- We refuse to allow *"our programs to take precedence over our purpose."* We do not talk about programs in our fellowship. Every member and every ministry is encouraged to keep a focus on our purpose statement. Ineffective, dated programs are replaced with ministry that is honoring to the Lord. Our church will not allow the "tail to wag the dog." We have a ministry plan that the Lord is blessing richly, and we intend to stay with it until He moves us.

- The illusion *"the eighty-twenty rule is the norm"* is being challenged regularly. We have learned that if you expect only twenty people out of one hundred to minister, then that is what you get. Recently, our church started an off-campus ministry (in Chesapeake). About one hundred committed members made up the core group. After receiving extensive training in areas such as Sunday School growth, Baptist doctrine, FAITH Evangelism, *The BodyLife Journey*, and general administrative duties, this group launched on October 1, 2000. Within three months the core group doubled, and the rented space was overflowing. The key was expectation — every member of the core group and new members of this campus *will* be involved. Signs of the fever of excitement are beginning to be seen at our central campus, too. God is reviving His people for the work of ministry.

- The opinion that *"belonging to a local church is not important"* continues to be challenged with example after example of members who say membership is vitally important. Members of every race, gender, and age are joining hands to accomplish ministry in Jesus' name.

I would be untruthful if I said that all of our members are connected. They are not. We may not be able to change the thinking of every one of the first several thousand members. But if the Lord wills, we will make an impact on the next several thousand members whom we are going to reach in His saving name.

Second, *expect to make several acclimatization sorties.*

Don't believe that thin-air mountaineers just walk to the top of the world. It takes several years of planning *before* they arrive at the base camp. Then each climber expects to be on the mountain for as long as two months. During that time, each climber ascends toward the summit of Everest by taking acclimatization sorties, short trips which are 1000 feet higher than the camp they are staying in that night. Sometimes they remain at these camps for days, until their bodies adjust to the high altitudes.

130

The same is true for the body of Christ. Change takes time, so the wise pastor will plan for that time. But be encouraged because every step your church takes toward bagging each of these mythological summits is a step for a healthy future in your church. The pace at which your church climbs depends on the spiritual fitness of that body of believers. Move too quickly and your people may lose sight of their spiritual guide; move too slowly and they may become discouraged and desire to remain halfway up the mountain. Mark each step forward as a victory for Jesus and enjoy, yes, even celebrate every victory!

Third, *involve as many people as possible for the journey.*

Start by preaching or teaching a series of messages on the myths of membership. Treat the information in this book as you might a menu in a restaurant. If you see something you don't like, you don't get up and leave the table. Instead, pick something you enjoy and order it. That's true for these chapters, too. As Adrian Rogers wisely states, "If these bullets fit your gun, then shoot them."

Investigate the materials called *The BodyLife Journey: Guiding Believers into Ministry.* They are designed to help a church of any size to correctly assimilate members into meaningful membership and personal ministry. Encourage every Sunday School leader, every deacon, every committee member, and any other key leader of your church to walk through *The BodyLife Journey* process with you. Remember if you build a fire, people will come and watch it burn. Finally, make me the bad guy when discussion times arise. Agree where you can and modify where you like. Conform your journey to your people.

Fourth, *invite the Holy Spirit alongside you for encouragement.*

Before a climber begins his trek up the face of Everest, he joins the Sherpas in a religious service. Buddhist prayer flags flap in the breeze as these natives offer prayers on behalf of the team. Climbing a mythological mountain demands supernatural power. With His encouragement, you will keep going when others want to quit. Keep your focus and stay close to Jesus.

Enjoy the trip. May these thrilling illustrations of reaching the summit inspire you to reflect and cry out like Caleb of old, "Give me this mountain!" Remember, the greatest risks in life are the ones not taken. After you have bagged a few of these summits, the Lord may give you a hunger and a passion to conquer additional mythological mountains.

See you at the top!

> *For truly I say to you, if you have faith as a mustard seed, you shall say to this mountain, "Move from here to there," and it shall move; and nothing shall be impossible to you* (Matthew 17:20).

CHRISTIAN GROWTH STUDY PLAN

Preparing Christians to Serve

In the **Christian Growth Study Plan (formerly Church Study Course),** this book ***REDEFINING CHURCH MEMBERSHIP: FROM MYTH TO MINISTRY*** is a resource for course credit in the subject area **CHURCH LEADERSHIP** of the Christian Growth category of diploma plans. To receive credit, read the book, complete the learning activities, show your work to your pastor, a staff member or church leader, then complete the information on the next page. The form may be duplicated. Send the completed page to:

Christian Growth Study Plan
One LifeWay Plaza
Nashville, TN 37234-0117
FAX: (615)251-5067
E-MAIL: *cgspnet@lifeway.com*

For information about the Christian Growth Study Plan, refer to the current Christian Growth Study Plan Catalog. It is located online at *www.lifeway.com/cgsp.* If you do not have access to the Internet, contact the Christian Growth Study Plan office (800.968.5519) for the specific plan you need for your ministry.

Redefining Church Membership
Course No. LS-0017

Social Security Number (see note below for option)

Date of Birth (Month, Day, Year)

Name (First, Middle, Last)

Home Phone

Address (Street, Route, or P.O. Box)

City, State, or Province

Zip/Postal Code

Please check appropriate box: ☐ Resource purchased by self ☐ Resource purchased by church ☐ Other

CHURCH INFORMATION

Church Name

Address (Street, Route, or P.O. Box)

City, State, or Province

Zip/Postal Code

CHANGE REQUEST ONLY

☐ Former Name

☐ Former Address

City, State, or Province

Zip/Postal Code

☐ Former Church

City, State, or Province

Zip/Postal Code

Signature of Pastor, Conference Leader, or Other Church Leader

Date

*New participants are requested but not required to give SS# and date of birth. Existing participants, please give CGSP# when using SS# for the first time. Thereafter, only one ID# is required. **Mail to:** Christian Growth Study Plan, One LifeWay Plaza, Nashville, TN 37234-0117. Fax: (615)251-5067.

Rev. 3-03